QUICK AND EASY

Vests

&Jackets

QUICK AND EASY

Vests & Jackets

KATE MATHEWS

Creative Fashions to Sew

LARK BOOKS

Art Director: Dana Irwin

Photography: Richard Babb

Illustrations: Pete Adams, Lisa Mandle, Bernadette Wolf

Production: Hannes Charen, Dana Irwin

Editorial Assistance: Val Anderson, Catharine Sutherland

Library of Congress Cataloging-in-Publication Data

Mathews, Kate.

    Quick and easy vests and jackets : creative fashions to sew / by Kate Mathews.—1st ed.

    p. cm.

    "A Lark sewing book."

    Includes index.

    ISBN 1-57990-056-9 (hard)

1. Vests.   2. Jackets.   3. Coats

TT615. M38   1999

646.4'5—dc21   98-22045

                                  CIP

10 9 8 7 6 5 4 3 2 1

First Edition

Published by Lark Books

50 College St.

Asheville, NC 28801, US

Distributed by Random House, Inc., in the United States, Canada, the United Kingdom, Europe, and Asia

Distributed in Australia by Capricorn Link (Australia) Pty Ltd., P.O. Box 6651, Baulkham Hills Business Centre, NSW 2153, Australia

Distributed in New Zealand by Tandem Press Ltd., 2 Rugby Rd., Birkenhead, Auckland, New Zealand

The written instructions, photographs, designs, patterns, and projects in this volume are intended for the personal use of the reader and may be reproduced for that purpose only. Any other use, especially commercial use, is forbidden under law without written permission of the copyright holder.

Every effort has been made to ensure that all the information in this book is accurate. However, due to differing conditions, tools, and individual skills, the publisher cannot be responsible for any injuries, losses, or other damages that may result from the use of the information in this book.

Printed in the United States

ISBN 1-57990-083-6

CONTENTS

6
Introduction

10
GET READY...By Taking Inventory

■ Build efficiency into your sewing area, for maximum results

■ Fit sewing into your schedule, and get more done

■ Take stock of your wardrobe, and sew to fill the gaps

22
GET SET...By Getting Inspired

■ Let the world around you inspire great new sewing ideas

36
GET READY...GET SET...SEW!

■ Streamline sewing for optimum efficiency

■ Use creative finishing touches to express your personal style

45
The Vests and Jackets

■ How-to instructions for adding pizzazz to a standard pattern and a Plan for the Week to organize construction for efficiency

124
About the Designers

126
Acknowledgments

128
Index

INTRODUCTION

Vests, jackets, and coats are the unsung heroes of our wardrobes, unifying, amplifying, and diversifying many different types of clothing. We wear certain kinds of vests, jackets, and coats over clothes to protect us from the elements. We also wear these items to accent a dress, tie together a skirt and blouse, or give new appeal to an old ensemble. Vests and jackets can unify different colors, fabrics, and textures to create a singular outfit that is unique to your personal style and sense of fashion. They can also harmonize unrelated articles of clothing into a perfectly orchestrated outfit. This book is designed to help you create a collection of distinctive and attractive vests, jackets, and coats to wear for a variety of occasions with a wide range of clothing.

FROM FUNCTIONAL TO FUNKY

Outer garments run the gamut from functional to fashionable to frivolous—and all points in between. Vests, jackets, and coats offer the versatility that you need to be able to dress yourself both stylishly and comfortably in all types of weather.

On the functional side are vests, jackets, and coats that protect us from sun, rain, cold, wind, and snow. No matter how you're planning to spend the day and no matter what you've chosen to wear, there's a good chance you'll be putting on some kind of outerwear. This is true whether you're going to the office, supermarket, or beach. The great news is that protective garments can be great looking, and we're going to show you designs and techniques for jazzing up these types of clothes.

In the mid-range are the less functional and more fashionable vests and jackets that you might wear all day long, either in the work place or at home, as part of your outfit for the day. You might combine a skirt or pants with a blouse and vest, or with a blazer, or you may decide to wear a smartly-styled jacket over a one-piece dress. Daytime vests and jackets offer marvelous opportunities for you to play with color, style, and embellishments, and let you show off your ingenuity while still achieving their basic objectives. This book is full of fantastic vests and jackets that you can make easily and quickly.

At the other end of the scale are vests, jackets, and coats that push the fashion envelope. We're going to show you many creative ways that you can embellish an ordinary vest and transform it into a unique piece of wearable art— just the right thing to wear to a party or concert.

THE GREAT ABYSS

How often have you stood in front of your open closet and been unable to find anything to wear? Some garments are too small, others need mending, and still others look kind of "blah." Nothing is just right. You realize (once again!) that you really must do something about your wardrobe to give it some more pizzazz. What can you do, given that time and money are always in very short supply?

You can't afford a whole new wardrobe, and you really don't want or need one anyway. You have plenty of perfectly good clothes that you'd be happy to wear if only you had something new to wear them with. There's that wonderful gray wool suit that you invested in when you got your first job out of college;

it will never go out of style. Although the jacket is too small, couldn't the skirt be rescued? Then there's the ever-so-comfortable pair of black trousers; if only you had something special to complement them. You think back to the gorgeous jacket you tried on last week at that trendy boutique; the fabric was luxurious, the collar doubled back on itself, and oh, the buttons were outrageous! It even came with a coordinated vest. Both would be great additions to your wardrobe, even if you have to live on peanut butter sandwiches for a month and sacrifice movies for a year.

Fed up, you grab a skirt and blouse, close the closet door firmly behind you, and mutter something about going to the store and looking through pattern books. Maybe you'll get an idea for a simple skirt or dress that you can "whip up" in the next few weeks. You start to feel better at once.

Hold it right there, please. We know you love to sew. But

before you rush out, buy a dress pattern, and stay up sewing every night for a week, consider this: a decision to devote next weekend to making just one new vest or jacket can add more depth and range to your wardrobe than a decision to spend the same weekend making another blouse, dress, or pair of pants. As you'll see when we get to the project section of this book, you can find the time to create vests, jackets, and coats that really will enhance and expand your wardrobe.

PUT YOUR VALUABLE RESOURCES TO THE BEST POSSIBLE USE

You probably think that finding opportunities in your hectic life to spend quality time with your sewing machine ranks up there as a sort of "mission impossible." This need not be the case. To help you make the most efficient use of your time, we've assembled a huge banquet of ideas and suggestions for efficient and time-saving sewing, and we've garnished them with a healthy dollop of new approaches to using your innate creativity in innovative ways. For most of the designer projects, we've compiled a slew of strategies for planning your schedule based on weekly outlines. You'll learn how to make the most practical use of weekday evenings, lunch hours, and odd moments during the day, in order to have enough time to assemble and finish a new garment over the weekend.

You'll also learn how to organize your wardrobe and your sewing area to utilize sewing resources to maximum efficiency and advantage, and you'll learn about the importance of selecting styles that complement your own body shape. Tips and strategies are presented for efficiently stitching and assembling your garments. You'll find out how easy it is to add the unique designer touches and embellishments that make clothing distinctive and exciting. Soon you'll be able to chart and navigate a direct course to spectacular finished garments in no time flat.

Because vests, jackets, and coats tend to be worn more frequently, you can definitely justify investing extra time, effort, and materials. It's well worth spending a bit more money on better quality fabrics and special buttons. It's also worth spending the time on a more complicated sewing technique. Consider adding piped edges or pocket welts, stitching some fancy overlays, or including other unusual details that will make a garment truly unique.

We hope the garments in these pages will inspire you to jazz up your wardrobe of basic skirts, pants, blouses, and dresses. You're probably already at least familiar with most of the techniques presented, and have likely tried a few once or twice in the past, either on your own or while taking a sewing class along the way. Here, however, the focus is on taking these basic techniques to the next level by practicing them in new ways. Once you understand the design approach and learn to do the technique, you'll be

able to enhance any garment with the greatest of ease. Some of the sewing techniques in this book were developed by the designers, but most are fairly standard ones that have been adapted to meet a particular need of the fabric or to give the garment a particularly unique look and style.

We're very excited about this collection of vest, jacket, and coat designs. You'll find that page after page is chock full of innovative styles, unusual combinations of fabrics, and unique special touches that are sure to get your creative juices flowing. Most of these garments probably don't look like any you've ever seen before, either on another person or hanging on a rack in a store. That's because each of them was individually created to meet specific design objectives and preferences. This is one of the secrets of individual style. Sure, go ahead and look at the latest fashions and fashion trends, but be sure to adapt them to your own personality and overall lifestyle. As these designers illustrate, the best designs are those that incorporate various combinations of fabric, color, and texture in ways that reflect and enhance the wearer's own style.

Looking through these photographs and sketches will give you many ideas about what might look good on you and what might help you get more use out of the skirts, pants,

blouses, and dresses you already own. Deciding to add one of these unusual vests or jackets to an ordinary skirt and blouse combination or on top of a "just-okay" dress might make all the difference in the world.

Feel free to adapt the projects to suit your own personal tastes, requirements, and whims. Consider these projects as a smorgasbord of ideas: help yourself to as much as you like, and don't be bashful about taking second helpings! By making use of the time-saving strategies presented here, you'll discover that you, too, can quickly make a spectacular new garment by next Monday morning, and show off a terrific outfit that combines the best of the old with something special and new.

GET READY...

By Taking Inventory

Any good project manager worth her salt will tell you that a comprehensive status report is indispensable when it comes to figuring out where you stand. Only then can you determine what you still need to obtain or do in order to achieve your goals. We're going to apply the same principle to the three primary aspects of sewing activities: your sewing area, your schedule, and your wardrobe. We'll examine each of these in turn and look at how to assess what you already have, how to compare it with what you need, and how to resolve the differences. First we'll look at your sewing area and how to make it more efficient, then we'll move on to your schedule and how to make the most of your time, and finally we'll consider the state of your wardrobe and how to get the most fashion value from your garments. Once you get all three aspects acting in harmony, you'll be able to cruise through your sewing projects without missing a beat.

WHERE DO YOU SEW?

The truly lucky ones among us actually have a special place in the house or apartment that is devoted exclusively to sewing activities. It may be an entire room, even if a small one, or it may only be part of a room that you can dedicate to your fabrics, patterns, books, magazines, notions, and other supplies and equipment. Here, your sewing machine and ironing board are always set up and ready to go at a moment's notice. Racks or rods have been installed to hang garments-in-progress or clothes that need mending or alteration. Plenty of sunlight floods the room, and green plants brighten the atmosphere and keep the air fresh. This kind of sewing area is a dream come true, and we continually hear it calling to us as we wash the breakfast dishes, drive the kids to music lessons, pull weeds in the garden, or daydream during a sales presentation. If we could just figure out how, we would eagerly give up many less-important activities to spend as much time as possible working on our latest sewing project in this beautiful space.

Most of us wind up arranging a sewing area on a more makeshift basis. We keep fabrics on a few shelves in the linen closet, store patterns on a bookshelf in the family room, keep spools of thread in the bottom drawer of the china closet, and commandeer the kitchen table between meals. Trying to maintain a steady rhythm while working a sewing project through to completion under these circumstances can be difficult, but we have learned to make do with what we've got. Even so, there are many small adjustments that can be made to improve things.

An organized office helps you be more efficient at work, and an organized kitchen helps you cook meals more efficiently. In the same way, getting your sewing area as organized as possible, whether centralized or not, is a fundamental principle of more efficient sewing. The first thing to do is take a good, hard look at exactly what you already have for sewing space.

If everything is pretty much in one place, try sitting down on the floor in the middle of the room to get a new perspective. Start by drawing a rough diagram of the room, indicating the locations of major items, such as cutting table, desk, sewing machine, shelves, racks or rods for hanging, and filing cabinet. As you examine your environment, make notes about what you like and what you don't like about the space. Would it be better to place your desk closer to the window? Would positioning your sewing machine next to the shelves make it easier to reach small items as they are needed? Will you need an extension cord or extra electrical outlet if you decide to set up your ironing board in the east corner, instead of the north? Is there space behind the door to install a wardrobe rack or clothing rod? Where will you plug in your radio? And where can you safely set your coffee or tea without endangering nearby objects or precious fabric?

Your situation may be such that you simply cannot confine all your sewing gear in one room or area of the house. If this is the case, the same mapping exercise applied to your whole house or apartment will not only help you remember where everything is, but may inspire you to find more appropriate or logical places to keep your sewing gear. Sometimes we tuck things into corners that make sense at the moment, but then can't remember exactly where we put them when we need them.

So, clipboard and pencil in hand, draw a rough sketch of the floor plan of your whole abode, and mark down where you store your sewing machine, fabrics and linings, patterns, iron and ironing board, basket of tools, and all your other sewing items when they're not in use. As you cruise through the house, try to identify nooks and crannies you can use to consolidate more of your sewing equipment and supplies. Don't overlook the top shelf of the coat closet, an unused corner in your bedroom, or a section of the laundry room. Look for small areas that are presently unused or under-utilized. Make them work for you by creatively rearranging and relocating household items that you use less frequently to give yourself better and easier access to your sewing-related gear.

Perhaps you can empty one large closet and build some

TAKE AN INVENTORY OF YOUR WARDROBE PERIODICALLY AND MAKE ROOM FOR NEW FAVORITES.

floor-to-ceiling shelving inside, to create a more centralized storage location. When you acquire a new piece of fabric, a nifty new sewing aid, or a great new pattern, you will know where to stow it. If you can spare a walk-in closet, claim it as a mini-sewing room for yourself.

Whether you have the luxury of a sacred sewing sanctuary, or need a map of your entire house to remember where you keep all your sewing tools and supplies, you want to be able to bring it all together when you decide to launch a new sewing project. Always try to leave as much of your sewing area as ready and neat as possible. You'll gain the flexibility of being able to accomplish countless sewing-related tasks during the spare five- or ten-minute segments of your busy day.

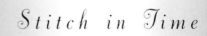

A Stitch in Time

Keep a small cache of office supplies within easy reach of the sewing machine, so you won't have to get up to fetch a pencil, eraser, or tape.

THE SAME SKIRT AND BLOUSE COMBINATION CAN LOOK CASUAL, CORPORATE, OR DRESSY DEPENDING ON THE CHOICE OF OVERGARMENT. WITH A FEW SPECIAL VESTS AND JACKETS, A LIMITED WARDROBE CAN PROVIDE UNLIMITED FASHION.

PLAN YOUR SPACE FOR MAXIMUM EFFICIENCY

Start from the premise that form proceeds from function. The form of a well-designed object (your sewing area, in this case) must stem from the purposes for which the object will be used. Each and every element of your sewing area must help, not hinder, your intent to begin and complete a multitude of sewing projects with the greatest of ease.

One key to being efficient is being able to find exactly what you need at exactly the moment you need it. Cubicles of all sorts, such as boxes, bins, baskets, crates, and drawers, are a great storage solution. See-through, stacking plastic shoe boxes are an inexpensive way to organize spools of thread, zippers, buttons and snaps, bindings, elastics, trimmings, needles, and other small tools

and sewing aids. Label the boxes and stack them on a bookshelf or in a cabinet. Many sewing shops sell handy cardboard boxes especially designed for storing patterns. To keep your favorite magazines conveniently at hand, purchase special notebook binders or plastic standing file boxes. Scour the stationery or office supply department at your local discount store for a variety of containers and cubicles of all shapes and sizes. Use them to organize all the elements of your sewing stash in a way that makes total sense to you and the way you live and sew.

KEEP YOUR SUPPLIES IN STOCK

Another key to being efficient is having as many of the supplies you might need on hand and ready to go to work. Use a sheet of paper or your computer to compile a

Master Inventory List of all the supplies you use regularly. Make a few copies and keep them on a clipboard hanging in your sewing area. Then you can easily circle, highlight, or check off those items that you will need to buy on your next shopping trip. If you notice that you're getting low on something or if you use the last of it, jot it down so you won't forget to buy more. Once a month or once a quarter, it's a good idea to take overall inventory of all your sewing supplies and plan a shopping trip specifically to replace what's low or depleted. This will help your budget-planning, too, because you'll be able to estimate on a regular basis how much money must be set aside for supply purposes.

While you're making up the Master Inventory List, take some time to prepare a Master Project Inventory List that can be used as a checklist when you start each new sewing project. Then you'll have a designated place to keep notes about the specific tools and supplies you'll need just for that project, and you won't forget the unusual items, such as collar stays or a frog closure.

S E W   O N   T H E   G O

Whether you take the centralized or the decentralized approach to organizing your sewing area, put together a mobile sewing station that you can roll or carry around the house as needed to a convenient working location. You may decide to do different sewing tasks in the living room, the kitchen, or the sun room, depending on the activity, the weather, or your mood that day. The mobile station can be a rolling cart with drawers, a picnic basket, a fishing tackle box, a set of stacking milk crates with casters attached, or even a suitcase on wheels. It's intended for your basic sewing tools, equipment, and supplies. You may wish to use a separate container to carry the pattern, fabric, thread, buttons, trims, and other items that are specific to your current project. When you're ready to work on your

YOUR PERSONAL STYLE MAY BE MULTI-FACETED, RANGING FROM CORPORATE TO CLASSY TO CASUAL.

latest creation, scan your Master Project Inventory List to make sure that everything you need is together in one spot as you move about the house. This simple idea can save you from running upstairs or downstairs for a spool of thread, your scissors, or a measuring tape.

Other storage suggestions for organizing your sewing area include making use of rolling carts, stacking bins, pegboards, picnic baskets, office filing cabinets, children's toy boxes, and camping storage boxes. You can find many handy storage devices and ideas at your local sewing shop, but don't overlook what's available at hardware stores, home improvement centers, camping supply stores, and through mail order catalogs.

If you need shelving, but can't afford to buy or have a carpenter build you nice wooden shelves, consider the steel shelving available in the hardware department of many department stores or at home improvement centers. Not only is it inexpensive, but steel shelving makes it possible to adjust the heights of the shelves to suit your needs, and later, rearrange those heights if your needs change. Steel shelves usually come in a lovely designer shade of industrial gray, but sometimes you can find them in red, black, or white.

Set up a travel tote to keep near your car keys, and take it with you whenever you leave the house. You never know when you'll be stuck in a major traffic tie-up or waiting room, needing something to do with your hands. Keep the tote stocked with needles, thread, pins, extra buttons, scissors, and note paper and pens. Then, add those small

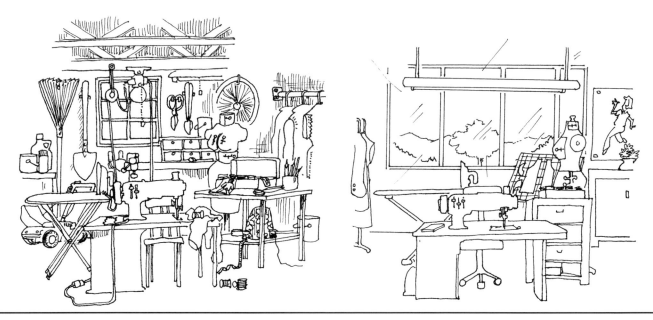

To make sure you sew, set up your gear wherever you can, from the garage to a sun-filled studio.

sewing and mending projects that you can get done without a whole lot of fuss when you have a few minutes to fill.

Search out new ideas

Yet another key to building more efficiency into your sewing area is to always be on the lookout for new ideas and new ways of doing things, and be willing to try something new to see if it works for you. When you go to the sewing store, take some time to look at new products that might have become available since you first learned to sew. You might be surprised to learn that someone finally did invent that handy little gadget you've been wishing for all these years, or to see that your store now carries an entirely new line of patterns, or to discover a convenient scissors-sharpening service. Take a moment to put your name on the store's mailing list. You'll find out about upcoming classes and sales on a regular basis, and will be able to integrate them into your schedule and budget ahead of time, instead of at the last minute.

Finally, be true to your own way of doing things. Change can indeed be exciting, but it's also time-consuming at the outset. Give new ideas a fair chance by trying them out, but settle on what works for you, not what works for your best friend. You might try her way, but give yourself permission to modify her ideas to suit your own idiosyncrasies. The most ingenious efficiency systems are useless unless you use them, and use them consistently. If you take

the time to learn, adapt, revise, and experiment until you come up with the perfect way for you, you'll find that, in the long run, you'll be spending much more of your time productively engaged in your favorite activity.

Where does all the time go?

There's so very much to do and so little time in which to get it all done. Despite new innovations and labor-saving devices, our lives today are filled to the brim with a wide range of personal, family, and professional activities and responsibilities. Technological advances that promised to shorten our work weeks and give us more leisure time are turning out to be a double-edged sword. The unabated pace of development has brought new activities and new issues into our lives that simply can't be ignored and must be accommodated.

A Stitch in Time

Stay up-to-date on the latest time-saving sewing tools and techniques by making a regular visit to your favorite sewing shop just to see what's new.

Generations of our foremothers did not have telephones, car phones, fax machines, computers, microwaves, or frozen dinners. Yet they seem to have lived much less hectic lives than we do. They had enough time to cook unprocessed foods, bake their own bread, enjoy face-to-face conversations with friends and family without the incessant ringing of the telephone or chatter from the TV set. They enjoyed the simple pleasure of writing and mailing a handwritten letter, content to live without instantaneous e-mail or overnight delivery. And they were able to find enough time in their day to sew and embellish beautiful garments, or take up fancy embroidery or quilting.

Today, most of us have so many work, family, and community obligations and activities that we often feel that someone or something is getting shortchanged. Even our free evenings feel over-scheduled. We wonder when we will ever get time to do something just for ourselves, that we truly enjoy. How will we ever find the time to sew?

PRIORITIZE, AND THEN SCHEDULE

Most of us must accept the fact that it's nearly impossible to set aside large chunks of unrestricted time during the week to start and finish a sewing project. What we need to do is figure out another approach, one that involves finding and using small windows of sewing time to get us ready to make the best use of whatever uninterrupted sewing time we manage to carve out of a busy week.

The simple secret is to prioritize sewing, just as you would an important meeting or appointment. If sewing is important to you, then you must elevate its status when you plan your daily, weekly, and monthly schedules. Instead of making yourself a vague promise to get some sewing done when you have a few spare minutes, try to give it as much importance as you give other high-priority

activities, such as grocery shopping, keeping a doctor's appointment, getting to class on time, or going to the school play. "Free time" will never magically appear in your life, so if you want to get any sewing done, then you must make appointments with yourself and schedule them into your calendar. Don't merely tell yourself that you'll look through some pattern books on your lunch hour on Tuesday; go ahead and write it in your daybook.

Finding ingenious ways to fit sewing into your busy life can become a pleasurable and rewarding game. By taking advantage of a few spare minutes here and there, every day, you'll be amazed at the multitude of small sewing-related tasks you can get done during the week. Then you'll be prepped and ready to spend the weekend cozied up with your sewing machine. It's the premise of this book that you can indeed learn to organize your next sewing project and your time so efficiently that you will be able to start and complete a new garment within the week. By making sure to get all the preparation tasks done during the week, you'll be free to concentrate on the actual assembly process on Saturday and Sunday.

The solution to the time crunch is to remember that sewing a garment involves far more than sitting down to stitch the pattern pieces together. A whole series of smaller tasks is required to produce a successful result. So when you start to look at your daily calendar or appointment book for available time, break down the larger activity of sewing into its component tasks, and then schedule time during the week to accomplish those tasks. For instance, you can set aside separate times to select and pretreat the fabric, study the pattern instructions, and complete the decorative embroidery on the collar pieces.

Of course, each of these activities can be even further divided into smaller and shorter sub-steps, many of which can be accomplished in a matter of minutes. When you sit down with your appointment book, rather than allocating 30 minutes on Monday afternoon to "sew," write down exactly which step or sub-step you plan to accomplish during that half-hour. If you feel a little unnerved about including sewing activities on an otherwise professional calendar, you can develop a personal code to use instead. You will be the only one who knows that "CP" means "cut out pattern," or that "PTF" means "pretreat fabric." Another approach is to use terms that are more common in a business setting. When you write "production planning," you will know that this is time you have set aside for taking inventory of supplies. When you see "R & D" scheduled for Wednesday afternoon, you know this means you have an appointment with some pattern books down at your local sewing store for some research and development.

With this kind of advance planning, you'll be able to

breeze through the week, thinking happy thoughts about your upcoming weekend date with yourself and your sewing machine. Most of the designer projects presented later in this book include a sample "Plan for the Week," to demonstrate how the designer arranged her own time to accomplish exactly these goals. You can easily do the same.

Take advantage of snippets of spare time

If you think about it, there are many unproductive moments every day that could be put to sewing-related use. Stitch a hem while waiting for the dinner casserole to bake. Visit the fabric store or sew buttons on your new jacket during a lunch hour. Doodle a new garment idea while talking on the telephone. Skim through a few fashion magazines while waiting in the grocery checkout line. Pick up needed items on your supply inventory list on your way home from work. Read pattern instructions while waiting for dinner to cook. Baste a seam while the iron heats up. Test some new fusibles while the bathtub fills.

This process works in reverse, too. While you're sewing a hem, you can also listen to a new book on tape, plan your next vegetable garden, or problem solve a work-related challenge. Just don't forget to pay attention to the main project at hand, the one that is, quite literally, in your hands.

Make the hard choices

Once you make the decision to get a new vest, jacket, or coat ready to wear by Monday morning, you will have to make some difficult choices about your leisure activities. This is what prioritizing is all about. You simply cannot do it all. Are you willing to give up that lunch date or evening out with friends? Can you choose to cut out the pattern instead of watching a video? Can you make a deal with your children to trade this Saturday afternoon's outing for one on the following Sunday? Only you can make these

A Stitch in Time

Set an alarm clock or wristwatch alarm to remind you when it's time to keep a date with your sewing machine.

choices. No matter how clever you are at finding ways to manage your time, you won't be able to get started if you're unable to make sewing a priority.

TAKE STOCK OF YOUR WARDROBE

Every woman dreams of a neatly-organized, well-stocked closet filled with good-fitting and smart-looking clothes, pairs upon pairs of stylish shoes, and a collection of smashing accessories that complement every outfit. All the colors are your colors, and all the styles fit you to perfection. Every garment combines beautifully with every other garment, and, except perhaps for a few oddball sentimental pieces, there is nothing hanging on the rods or folded on the shelves that you couldn't wear with confidence and aplomb. Within minutes, you can be dressed and ready to go, beautifully outfitted for any occasion and feeling on top of the world.

Sadly, this isn't the case for most of us. Instead, our closets have plenty of perfectly good clothes that we don't wear much anymore. Some don't fit quite right, some don't look quite right, and others just don't seem to go with anything else we have. In addition, most of us hold onto certain items for sentimental reasons, long after their "go-with" companions have disappeared.

We have all experienced the short-term satisfaction of cleaning out the clothes closet. We dutifully try on everything in front of a full-length mirror and exuberantly pile

PLAN EVERY DAY TO INCLUDE SEWING TASKS.

15 THINGS YOU CAN DO
in 15 Minutes

1. Check your current measurements and note any changes that will require pattern alterations.

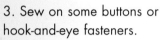

2. Try on different shoulder pads to see how they look with your new jacket.

3. Sew on some buttons or hook-and-eye fasteners.

4. Make a list of notions needed for your next project.

5. Study the pattern directions, and identify ways to streamline construction.

6. Chart out your schedule for the week and weekend.

7. Make some welts for jacket pockets.

8. Measure and mark the positions of buttonholes on a vest front.

9. Model your favorite outfit and decide why you like it so much.

10. Begin prewashing the fabrics and interfacing for your next project.

11. Look through your pattern collection for new ideas.

12. Play around with different appliqué arrangements on the back of an unfinished jacket.

13. Wind a dozen bobbins of your favorite neutral thread color.

14. Clean and oil your sewing machine.

15. Close your eyes and daydream about new fashions to sew.

For those of us who sew and who also experience wardrobe fatigue, it's tempting to decide to "whip up" a dress or skirt in the next few weeks so that we can have something new to wear. Although this may sound like an easy way out of the problem, it's actually setting ourselves up for more heartache in the future. Another simple skirt or dress doesn't address the problem, because we already have plenty of simple garments that may not coordinate with other items in the closet. The better solution is to take the time now to look critically at your wardrobe, in its entirety, and then determine what kinds of garments could help unify and diversify all the individual pieces.

By adding just a few new vests and jackets, the number of outfits that you can create with what is already hanging in your closet multiplies exponentially. For example, two tops (A and B) and two bottoms (C and D) can be combined in only four different ways: AC, AD, BC, and BD. Add one vest (V1) to each of the four combinations, and you now have a total of eight different outfits: the first four, plus ACV1, ADV1, BCV1, and BDV1.

Add another vest (V2), and you can now create a total of twelve different looks: the first eight, plus ACV2, ADV2, BCV2, and BDV2. The further addition of just one jacket (J) gives you a possible 24 different combinations. This is enough for you to dress for work for one entire month without having to repeat yourself.

See how easy this is? Just imagine if you have five or more vests and jackets at your disposal! And don't forget, you probably have more than two tops and two bottoms to start with. There is also no reason why you can't wear a jacket or vest over a dress. All you need to understand are some wardrobe basics and what kinds of vests, jackets, and coats will best suit you.

the questionables on the bed or floor. We decide what still fits and what doesn't, and set aside the rejects to pass along to a friend or donate to charity. Then we hang up the remaining garments in organized categories, according to style, color, or other preference. The truth is that now we've got a well-organized collection of garments that still don't add up to great-looking outfits that we're thrilled to wear.

If we are ever going to attain the nirvana of wardrobes, we must take a different approach by periodically taking serious stock of our wardrobes. Businesses do this all the time. Most manufacturers take inventory of their parts or supplies on a quarterly or yearly basis. Then they can compare what they have on hand with what they know they will need in the coming months. This seems like a logical way to approach a personal wardrobe. If you don't know what you have, you won't know what you need, whether you are planning to buy it, borrow it, or sew it for yourself.

A Stitch in Time

Instead of making lists or trusting your memory, use a small hand-held tape recorder to keep track of great ideas that come to you while driving, or anything else you don't want to forget.

UNDERSTANDING WARDROBE BASICS

The idea of a wardrobe is really very simple. At its heart, your core wardrobe consists of a personal collection of tops, bottoms, vests, jackets, dresses, and coats. Tops include blouses, sweaters, turtlenecks, and T-shirts; bottoms are your skirts, walking shorts, and pants; and dresses are one-piece stand-alone garments. Variations include jumpers, which require a top underneath, and suits, which combine a bottom, a top, and a jacket, with or without a vest. When you get dressed or change clothes, you simply choose one top and bottom combination, one dress or jumper combination, or one suit combination. These are essentially your only options for putting outfits together, and this fact alone should make getting dressed a whole lot easier.

"Okay," you say, "I get your point. But what you're describing sounds kind of boring, like ordering dinner at a Chinese restaurant where you choose one dish from Column A and two from Column B. I want to give my basic outfits a little pizzazz. I want to make them more 'me.' Can you help me with that?"

Yes, we certainly can. That's what this book is all about, helping you design vests, jackets, and coats quickly and easily, that work with your existing wardrobe and reflect your personal style. The secret is variety. How each woman chooses to use variety in her wardrobe is what gives her a unique sense of style. The French have a marvelous word for it: cachet (rhymes with sashay). Cachet refers to "a mark or quality of distinction," and it is truly worth including in your efforts to develop a more fashionable, yet still functional, wardrobe. The trick is to develop fashion cachet that is true to who you are and how you live your life. The garments you choose must complement, facilitate, and enhance your lifestyle and look good while doing so. This is equally true whether you are cheering your child's soccer team, giving a presentation to the board of directors, sharing dinner with your significant other, doing research at the local university, or taking your cat to the vet. You always want to look remarkable, so the world can marvel at your cachet, even when you are just dashing into the market for milk and bread.

KNOW YOUR BEST COLORS

Do you know which colors look good on you? Do you know which colors don't? Do you find that people consistently compliment you when you're wearing your favorite red suit, or baby blue dress? This is a clue to which colors we should find when we look in the closet. If your hand consistently gravitates toward certain garments, one of the reasons probably has to do with its color. It's perfect for you. On the flip side, garments that never see the light of day may likely be in colors that are all wrong for you.

There are several color systems available through books, workshops, and color consultants, to help you determine what color groups are right for you, based on skin tones and hair color. If you choose to investigate them, you may gain some interesting insights into why you never wear certain garments and why others become well-worn favorites. Then you can put those lessons to work in the sewing room, as you consistently turn out new fashions that bring out the best in you.

IDENTIFY THE STYLES THAT FLATTER YOU

Yes, human bodies come in all shapes and sizes, varying dramatically in height, weight, and proportion. Of course, your unique shape and size have little to do with who you are on the inside. However, the way you dress has a great deal to do with how you perceive yourself and how other people perceive you, especially if they are strangers who don't know the "real you." If you look in the mirror and love what you see, then you will feel, and look, great from the inside out. A woman wearing an expensive, classically tailored, and impeccably accessorized wool suit conveys an entirely different impression than a woman wearing an equally expensive and impeccably accessorized silk ensemble purchased at an avant garde gallery of wearable art. Both women would convey yet another image if they wore jeans and T-shirts.

What impression do you want to convey? This leads us naturally into a consideration of garment style, not to be confused with personal style, or cachet. Garment style refers to its silhouette and design lines. For example, skirts can be A-line, full, pleated, straight, circle, or wraparound. Pants can be loose, tapered, pleated, cuffed, or bell-bottomed. Tops can be yoked, button-down, turtleneck, tailored, or raglan. Dresses can be princess, tent, empire, shirtwaist, or sheath. Vests can be tunic-style, bolero-style, fitted or loose, with or without a collar. Jackets can be single- or double-breasted, tailored or not, lined or unlined, and cropped short or hip-length. Coats can be fitted or loose, pleated or plain, flared or narrow, heavyweight or lightweight, and with or without shoulder pads.

Some of these styles will look great on you, others will look so-so, and still others will be downright unflattering. You'll know at a glance in the mirror which ones look best, and this knowledge makes it easier to steer clear of fashion failures. If you don't trust your own eyes, visit your library and study the many books that can help you determine the best garment styles for your particular figure. Then, you can effectively choose patterns and fabrics to create or enhance the look you want to achieve.

EMBRACE THE Q FACTOR

Simply stated, the "Q Factor" is that aspect of your wardrobe that makes an emphatic statement about the uniqueness of you. It's a type of trademark, and is first cousin to cachet. The Q Factor is something you become

ORGANIZE YOUR SUPPLIES AND KEEP A LIST OF OUT-OF-STOCK ITEMS, SO YOU'LL HAVE WHAT YOU NEED.

A Stitch in Time

Make the active choice to give sewing a higher priority in your life. If you don't make the time for sewing, no one else will do it for you.

A Stitch in Time

Successful business people know the
value of the axiom "Plan your work and
work your plan." Make this wisdom work
for you and your sewing goals.

known for; it's part of your fashion reputation, a signature theme or item of some sort. For example, your Q Factor might be wearing something teal-colored every day, or changing the heirloom stickpin in the lapel of your business suit every day.

When applied to your wardrobe, the Q Factor could mean that you only wear a certain style skirt, or that you always wear a vest, or that you are never seen in public without a hat. It's entirely up to you to decide whether, and how, to make the Q Factor part of your personal style. Once you have embraced the Q Factor as a fundamental part of everyday life, people will surely recognize you because of it, and notice its absence.

EXPLORE THE POSSIBILITIES

Much like separating the wheat from the chaff, a great rule of thumb to use when evaluating the potential of your wardrobe is to separate the spectacular from the ordinary. What sets it apart? If you study the photographs throughout this book, you will see that the fabulous is often found in the details. Ordinary garments offer nothing special to the eye, while spectacular garments showcase interesting accents, eye-catching details, and other unusual features. If you take the time to explore your options and add just one offbeat or unexpected touch to your next sewing project, the unconventional result will be well worth the extra effort. You will have created a garment that reflects the essence of you and gets noticed every time you wear it.

DETERMINE WHAT YOU WANT

Once you know a bit more about the styles and colors that help you look your best, you can then spend your valuable time creating garments that guarantee a successful look. You've read the books, studied your favorite fashions, and looked critically at yourself and your clothes in the mirror. You've examined your lifestyle requirements and identified

the most compatible types of garments and fabrics. You have pruned your wardrobe down to those items that fit perfectly, are styled to accentuate your best features and minimize problem areas, and can be worked into any number of wonderful outfits.

Now it's time to identify those items in your closet that could tie together with a vest or jacket. As you look through your pattern and fabric stash, you will be able to imagine how a particular vest or jacket would look with specific clothes you already own. For example, you might have a beautiful green paisley skirt that fits perfectly, but that you haven't worn since the only blouse you can wear with it is torn in the front. Sure, you mended it, but you still don't feel right wearing the blouse in public. Instead of finding new homes for both the skirt and the blouse, dip into your fabric collection and make a stunning new jacket or vest that will cover the mend and give you a whole new outfit.

As you study the photographs and projects in this book, with your own wardrobe in mind, you will see how a simple but creative approach to sewing can help you pull together the disparate elements in your closet, multiply and diversify your outfits, and give ordinary garments extraordinary fashion appeal.

GET SET....

By Getting Inspired

By now, you have done much of your homework. You've scrutinized your wardrobe to determine what's a keeper and what's not. You've figured out what fits and what doesn't. You've decided what you should keep, what you should give away, and what you should alter or modify into a more suitable garment that fits your personal style and wardrobe. You've taken the time to analyze your body shape, and you now know which design features will accentuate your positive attributes and which will minimize less-than-ideal characteristics. You've looked at your schedule with a critical eye and made a serious commitment to yourself to make sure you don't let your sewing dreams wither on the vine for lack of nurturing.

INFUSE YOURSELF WITH INSPIRATION

Just before you start on a new project is the time to open your eyes and mind to new ideas. Ideas come in all shapes, sizes, and colors. They are around you all the time; you simply need to notice them. They show up in daydreams, as well as in night dreams. You never know when you'll turn a corner and encounter a great new idea. It may be an offbeat color combination, a refreshingly different collar shape, an unusual appliqué design, or any of a hundred good ideas for your next project. Coming up with creative ideas doesn't require any special talent. If something you notice seems like a great possibility for innovation, trust your intuition. It will never fail you.

There are many ways to stimulate the development of fresh ideas. Take a class, even if it's not sewing-related. Just being around other creative people is invigorating. Go to the local shopping mall or downtown boulevard and watch people. Take note of what they are wearing, what looks great, and what doesn't. Note the styles and details that catch your eye, and why. Watch an exotic foreign-language film and don't read the subtitles; you'll notice a

DESIGNER SHEILA BENNITT FRAMES A BASIC BLACK DRESS WITH A QUICK-TO-MAKE VEST AND TWO COORDINATING NECK/HEAD WRAPS THAT CAN BE WORN IN MANY DIFFERENT WAYS. SERGING THE RAW EDGES OF THE DRAPEY FABRIC CREATES AN INTERESTING RUFFLED EFFECT AND TAKES JUST MINUTES TO DO.

great deal about the costume and set design. Go to the zoo, by yourself or with young friends, and marvel at the magnificent colors and designs in feathers and fur. Spend an hour in an art museum studying any large oil painting that catches your eye. Stand further back and take in the whole, then get up close and see how the painter combined delicate brush strokes in different colors to achieve the desired effect. Think about how you can do the same thing with fabric or thread. Spend several minutes studying a single flower to see what you can learn about symmetry and color. Study the world around you and you'll be amazed at the creative possibilities of color, texture, and pattern.

Don't forget to look in the obvious places for sewing inspiration, such as fashion and sewing magazines, boutiques, pattern books, fabric stores, mail-order catalogs, and home decorating journals. Talk sewing with a friend or attend a lecture. Get online and enjoy the visually stimulating web sites. When you're in any type of store for any reason whatsoever, be on the lookout for new color combinations, fabric types, and embellishment ideas. They might be hiding incognito in the furniture, bedding, jewelry, or garden department.

Take your inspiration from wherever you find it. Don't limit yourself in your search for a fresh approach. More often than not, truly innovative design ideas come from left field, the unexpected source. So keep your eyes open and your senses well-tuned to the world around you. Just be sure to carry your trusty note pad, pens, and measuring tape, so you will be prepared to record any and all good ideas. Taking along a camera or hand-held tape recorder is also a good idea, so you can document your observations while going about your business, without having to remember everything later.

WATCH THE WORLD GOING BY AND ADAPT INNOVATIVE IDEAS TO YOUR OWN LIFESTYLE.

What's the point of such staged exercises? You'll find that many of your observations can be jumping off points for new sewing designs. When you start raising your consciousness about fashion and sewing, you'll come up with more ideas than you'll ever have time to sew.

BUILD YOUR OWN INSPIRATION REFERENCE LIBRARY

Over the years, you've probably collected at least a few books on sewing, some magazines, and perhaps more than a small stack of loose articles about new sewing techniques. You might have one or more file folders of clippings, sketches, and photographs of ideas that you've been saving for the future. All these resources won't do you much good if they're scattered throughout the house, hidden away in a filing cabinet, or stacked in a corner gathering dust.

So, round up all these gems, sort them out, and organize them. Use a three-ring binder or file folders to create a new home for all the loose pieces of paper. Tack some sketches, swatches, and photos up in plain sight on an "Inspiration Bulletin Board." Arrange all your sewing-related books and magazines on an "Inspiration Bookshelf." Store your three-ring binders there, too, as well as your collection of sewing patterns and instructional videos. By grouping all these reference materials in one very visible

A Stitch in Time

Don't be afraid to let your creativity run wild, and see where it takes you. You don't have to sew every idea you come up with, just the great ones.

place, you will be able to draw on them when you're searching for that special something or perfect finishing touch for a sewing project.

Regularly add new items to your inspiration library and change the selection on the bulletin board. This will refresh your perspective, and you may see details or possibilities you didn't notice before. This is a simple method of prodding yourself to look at things in a new way.

TAKE A FIELD TRIP

A wonderful, and enjoyable, hands-on approach to rejuvenating your idea supply is to visit a nearby department store (the more expensive, the better) and try on a variety of garments. When you get dressed for this educational

MAKE A FIELD TRIP TO THE DEPARTMENT STORE FOR NEW FASHION IDEAS.

excursion, be sure to wear clothing that you can take off and put back on without too much fuss, and shoes that you can slip in and out of easily. A good bet is to wear a leotard and tights under your outer clothes. And don't forget to take a notebook, pencil, and tape measure, so you can record what you learn.

Try on all the types of garments that are available in the category in which you are interested. If you want to

A Stitch in Time

To experiment with colors and styles, make a paper doll from a photo of yourself and dress her with cutouts from the latest fashion magazines or sketches of your own design.

A simple pattern can be a perfect laboratory for creative experimentation, as in this vest by designer M. Luanne Carson, who created one front as a teaching aid for a pin-weaving class. Since she did not want the other front to be a perfect match, she had fun piecing a complementary fabricscape and carried it around to the vest back. By incorporating accents of the skirt fabric in the vest assemblage, she ended up with a perfectly coordinated outfit.

make a vest, try on tabards, tunics, jerkins, boleros, and anything else you can find. If you're considering making a jacket, try on the whole array of single-breasted, double-breasted, cardigan, peplum, and Chanel and blazer styles. Check out ponchos, capes, cloaks, shawls, and cocoons. Consider the military, motorcycle, hunting, and fishing styles. Even though you might not be particularly interested in this last group, you might notice construction details that can be incorporated into a unique garment for yourself.

Try on your favorite styles in a variety of colors, from your basic navy, brown, and black to the more expressive colors that you might not otherwise consider wearing. Examine the differences in length, color, texture, and fabric. What looks great? What leaves you cold? Make notes or draw quick sketches that describe the most promising styles or details. This is valuable research that you can refer to when you're working on your own originals.

Simplicity can be profoundly memorable. This elegant and dramatic evening fashion by designer Lisa Mandle makes a lasting impression with just two fabrics: a luscious chocolate brown velvet and some well-chosen accent fabrics.

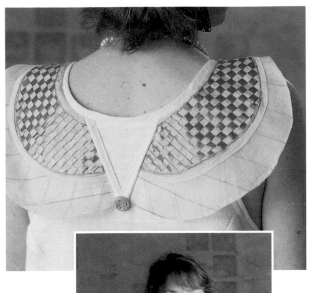

Let an interesting material be the center of attention, by choosing uncomplicated garment styles that don't interfere too much with the fabric pattern. In this jacket by designer Lisa Mandle, the fabric is showcased and all that is needed to top it off are some special buttons.

This lightweight, summery style by designer Lisa Mandle can be worn by itself or as a tunic vest over another garment. Some artful attention to the back collar makes a truly original statement.

Uncomplicated garment designs will stand out from the crowd when finished off with interesting textures and subtle shaping, as in the pretty collar and cuffs of this jacket and dress ensemble by designer Lisa Mandle.

When you're overwhelmed by the daily grind, stand in front of your inspiration bulletin board and drink in the good ideas you see.

FREEDOM TO FLY

When you finally start to bring creative ideas to life in your own custom garments, don't hesitate to experiment. Remind yourself that you are not obligated to use a new idea exactly as is. Modify it, adapt it to suit your individual style or personal preferences, and make it your own. The designers' ideas presented in these pages are meant to stimulate your own creative juices and get you motivated to sew. Feel free to fly, and see where you go!

THE VERY SAME PATTERN CAN LOOK COMPLETELY DIFFERENT, DEPENDING ON THE FABRIC YOU CHOOSE. FOR THESE VESTS BY DESIGNER JUDITH ROBERTSON, THE NATURAL LINEN PROVIDES A TAILORED AND CRISP LOOK, WHILE THE ABSTRACT RAYON PRINT VERSION IS ARTISTIC AND DRESSY.

DESIGNER M. LUANNE CARSON GIVES A CLASSIC BLACK EVENING DRESS A SURPRISING TWIST WITH THIS EASY COW PRINT VEST AND ITS UNCONVENTIONAL BUCKLE. SUCH A SIMPLE-SEW GARMENT CAN BE FUN TO WEAR AND CAN'T HELP BUT MAKE EVERYONE SMILE.

Designer Mary Cissell Lucas combined a handwoven fabric she didn't particularly like with some luck, chance, and an open mind. When cut into strips, rewoven, and accented with some novelty yarns, the fabric was transformed into this wonderful fashion she calls "Caterpillar's Nirvana Jacket."

Collaboration with another designer can yield extra-special results. For this "color study" vest, Mary Cissell Lucas wove three pieces of fabric and then turned them over to sewing designer M. Luanne Carson. Luanne arranged the color sections for the most interesting effect, created a freehand collar design, and positioned the naturally fringed selvage edge of the handwoven fabric at the lower edge as an "au naturale" hem.

Ingenious camouflage can extend the life of damaged fashions, unbeknownst to any observer. In this poncho jacket by designer Judith Robertson, the appliqué shapes cover up moth holes and use just a tiny amount of scrap fabric. Anyone would guess that this is the look the designer intended, instead of a creative cover-up.

Idea Notebook:

FINE AND FANCY FASTENERS

A plain garment can spring to life with something as simple as a clever closure.

A box jacket and the classic vest silhouette are quick and easy to make, but can end up looking boring and predictable. You don't have to redesign a whole garment to give it some pizzazz, as demonstrated by these ingenious ideas for changing the front fasteners. A simple alteration of the right and left front edges provides ample opportunity for creative variation. Then, add some attention-getting buttons or a mini-sculpture of beads and fabric to close the garment with singular style.

A SELF-FABRIC DRAPE ADDED TO ONE SIDE OF THIS FINISHED VEST ADDS SOME UNUSUAL FLAIR. THE END OF THE DRAPE IS GATHERED, TIED, AND DECORATED WITH COLORFUL BEAD DANGLES.
DESIGNER: JUDITH ROBERTSON.

A BUTTON WRAPPED WITH A SCRAP OF THE VEST FABRIC, TOPPED WITH A RED BEAD, CREATES A VISUAL FOCAL POINT FOR THIS ASYMMETRICAL-FRONT VEST. THE ACTUAL FASTENER IS A SNAP HAND-STITCHED BEHIND THE BUTTON.
DESIGNER: JUDITH ROBERTSON.

A PEARL BUTTON STITCHED ON WITH RED THREAD, TO BLEND WITH THE FABRIC'S PATTERN, MAKES A PERFECT CLOSURE. BUT THE DESIGNER TOOK THE IDEA FURTHER AND EMBELLISHED THE VEST LAPELS WITH A RANDOM ASSORTMENT OF BUTTONS. THE FINISHED GARMENT GETS PLENTY OF SURPRISED DOUBLE TAKES WHENEVER SHE WEARS IT. DESIGNER: JUDITH ROBERTSON.

A SLIGHT REDRAWING OF THIS VEST FRONT'S LOWER EDGE CRE-ATES AN INTERESTING ASYMMETRY AND THE PERFECT SETTING FOR TWO GREAT BUTTONS. DESIGNER: JUDITH ROBERTSON.

THE LEADING EDGE OF THIS VEST IS MADE MORE INTRIGUING BY ADDING A DUPLICATE SILHOUETTE. A SIMPLE IDEA THAT'S SIMPLE TO DO TURNS A NICE GARMENT INTO SOMETHING SPECIAL. DESIGNER: JUDITH ROBERTSON.

A BLACK SILK VEST BECOMES SO
MUCH MORE WITH A COORDINATED
ARRANGEMENT OF APPLIQUÉ SHAPES
AND A LINE OF TWO-TONE BUTTONS
THAT CONNECTED THE DESIGN FROM
SHOULDER TO HEMLINE.
DESIGNER: JUDITH ROBERTSON.

An alternative to stitching button loops into the seam is to overhand knot the ends of the loops and tack them to the surface. Designer: Judith Robertson.

Unusual wooden buttons lashed together by a decorative knot of suede lacing create a natural-looking fastener that's just right for this earth-toned tweed. A snap hidden behind the fastener keeps the wearer from having to re-tie the lacing each time. Designer: Judith Robertson.

By cutting off the front overlap, the edges can butt together, making this arrangement of buttons and loops possible. This is a great idea for creatively closing a reversible garment. Designer: Judith Robertson.

Idea Notebook:

DESIGN THEMES

For exciting and creative effects, focus your garment ideas around themes or subjects that are meaningful to you or have interesting design possibilities.

THIS JACKET DESIGN IS ONE OF A LITURGICAL SERIES BY MARY PARKER AND REPRESENTS THE SEASON OF PENTECOST. MACHINE STITCHED ON THE INSIDE FRONT FACINGS ARE THESE HIDDEN MESSAGES: GOODNESS, PEACE, GENTLENESS, JOY, FAITH, MEEKNESS, LOVE.

MARY PARKER CREATED THESE HIS-AND-HER VESTS FOR CAROLING DURING THE CHRISTMAS SEASON. ONE IS DECORATED WITH CHERUBIM, THE OTHER WITH SERAPHIM; EACH VEST HAS A SINGLE ANGEL ON ONE SHOULDER TO "WATCH OVER THE WEARER."

MARY PARKER'S JACKET FOR LENT USES THE BLACK AND PURPLE DISPLAYED IN HER CHURCH DURING THE LENTEN SEASON. SHE ALSO CUT SMALLER CROSS SHAPES OUT OF THE TAPESTRY FABRIC'S OVERALL DESIGN AND SATIN STITCHED THEM ON TOP OF THE SOLID COLORS TO FURTHER REINFORCE THE THEME.

Ideas for garment designs can come from jewelry, as these three fashions illustrate. For the jacket at left, Mary Parker chose a tartan-style plaid to set off the Scotsman pin. At center the jacket's striped fabric and zebra-print button were perfect mates for Mary Parker's zebra pin. At right, Luanne Carson purchased a special pin by North Carolina artist Sandy Webster and then waited for the perfect fabrics and vest design to come along.

If you're stumped for a new idea start your thinking from a specific theme or subject and then let your garment designs take off from there. Themes can be as simple as specific colors (shades of red), contrasts (black/white, dark/light, narrow/wide), or Mother Nature (landscapes, seascapes). A theme approach can also get a bit more complex, as in the liturgical garments of designer Mary Parker shown here. Whatever theme or subject you choose to develop, you can be sure the finished garments will showcase your originality.

As a lover of fabric and clothing, custom dressmaker Elizabeth Searle also appreciates designer clothing labels for their design potential. In this vest, she shows off a bevy of labels, including her own (Elizabeth Helene) covering the bottom button.

This vest by Sonia Huber is decked out with her personal collection of membership pins, tokens, childhood buttons, and other goodies. The designer says that this fun fashion is a conversation piece and also puts to good use all those high school pins, award charms, and souvenir patches stashed away in memento boxes.

GET READY, GET SET... SEW

You've been to the store and selected the perfect fabrics, returned home to pretreat them to prevent shrinkage and check for colorfastness, and scheduled your week to allow time for getting the garment ready to wear on Monday morning. You want to make sure that everything turns out just as you've imagined and planned. There are many ways to give yourself every possible advantage in seeing that this happens with as little frustration and as few mistakes as possible. Here are just a few of the many time-saving ideas about pattern selection, fitting, clothing construction, finishing, and embellishing that you can use to breeze through the process and prevent possible disaster.

SELECTING PATTERNS FOR EFFICIENCY AND CREATIVITY

Choose styles that complement and enhance your figure, that facilitate your lifestyle, and that offer appropriate challenges to your personal level of sewing expertise. It may be tempting to select a style that is shapeless and loose-fitting because you think it will be easier to sew or because you'll be able to skip the fitting step. But these are the very garments that you will end up never wearing.

Well-fitting fashions that define and move with the natural contours of your body are the ones that will become key components of your wardrobe.

Do choose basic patterns that are simply designed; simple styles will provide great opportunities for creative modification and variation. For example, a pattern style with straight side seams and no front darts provides a type of "blank canvas" on which you can create your own imaginative landscape. A pattern modified to be reversible offers a marvelous chance to double the mileage you can get from any one garment. You can sew two great designer originals for little more than the price or effort of one. Remember exponential value? It certainly applies to reversible fashions.

Just because you choose a particular pattern does not mean you have to use all its elements. It's perfectly all right to mix and match components from one pattern with another. For example, use the collar from a favorite jacket pattern to give

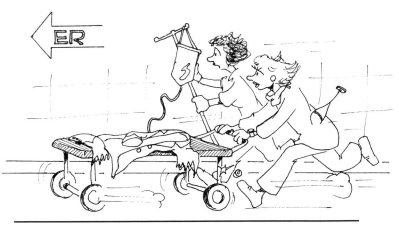
A Stitch in Time

Buttons and other innovative fasteners
can be miniature works of art, and will
transform an ordinary garment into an
extraordinary fashion original.

a different look to a tried-and-true vest pattern. Or take
advantage of the good fit of another jacket pattern and
make it without the sleeves for a flattering tunic vest. You'll
find that many pattern components can migrate quite nicely, even if a few minor changes are necessary to make the
pieces physically match up.

TAKE TIME TO ACHIEVE A PROPER FIT

In the long run, you won't be wasting time by spending
time to make sure your garments will indeed fit well. Don't
assume that the pattern size you selected based on the
manufacturer's measurement system will actually conform
to your own body shape. Few women match the pattern
companies' "standard" figures, so we all must be prepared
to individualize the patterns we use. It may be necessary
to adjust the entire pattern or some of its parts to meet
your own figure requirements. A good method for this is to
make a custom fitting pattern, also called a sloper, that
accurately fits your measurements. It's not a difficult
process, and you can learn the technique from any one of
a number of books available to you at the library, or by
taking a special class offered by your sewing shop, community college, or local Extension Service.

Alternatively, make a muslin test sample of the pattern
before you purchase or cut into the fashion fabric. This is a
great way to test the fit and feel of the actual pattern you
will be using, and it also offers opportunities for you to
experiment with pattern modifications or various decorative
stitches. You'll also have the advance opportunity to test
stitching techniques, machine tension, pleating depth, and
other aspects of the construction process. Once you make
the muslin garment, you can try it on with various other
items in your closet. This might spark new or additional
ideas about colors, textures, and special features that will
enhance the versatility of your overall wardrobe.

STUDY THE PATTERN BEFORE YOU START

To ensure that construction goes smoothly once you begin,
spend a few minutes reviewing the pattern instructions
ahead of time, no matter how many times you've previous-
ly used them. Highlight or note important steps along the
way or critical details you won't want to overlook as you
work your way through the process. Mark down any
design or construction changes you plan to make, so you
won't forget to do them at the proper time. Be alert to
aspects of the construction process that you may be less
familiar with, so you can refer to your library of tips and
techniques for helpful information.

Looking over the pattern guide sheets beforehand also
helps you identify steps that might be consolidated or completed in a slightly different order, to better match your
expertise level or working habits. For example, many patterns direct you to make the collar early in the process and
the cuffs later on, after you begin working on the sleeves.
Since both collar and cuffs involve the same stitch, clip,
press, and turn procedure, you'll save some time by doing

A Stitch in Time

Don't skimp on the pressing parts of
garment construction. Keep your iron
turned on so it's always ready when
you need it.

Good lighting in your sewing area will prevent eyestrain and fatigue. When you can see what you're doing, you'll fend off mistakes and stitching problems.

when you get to stitching steps later on, because the work-in-progress will be easier to handle. Also, your finished fashions will exhibit a professional touch that can never be recovered by trying to press the garment all at once after it's entirely sewn. You can, however, save pressing time by keeping the iron turned on all the time while you're working, being sure to top off the water level regularly. Also, if you lower your ironing board and position it right next to your sewing machine table, you won't even have to get up from your chair to press a seam.

INVENTION WAS THE MOTHER OF EFFICIENCY

Always be on the lookout for new supplies and equipment that will help you speed up the sewing process, and be willing to try them when an appropriate situation presents itself. When you're in your favorite sewing store, look for new tools for cutting, marking, basting, and stitching that you may not have noticed before. These time-saving devices can eliminate forever frustrations that you may

them together. Simply set the cuffs aside until you need them.

Use assembly-line principles to gain efficiency in your sewing, especially if you're planning to make two or three versions of the same basic garment, even if you're planning modifications to each one. Cut out the different garments at the same time and complete the construction steps one after the other. You might want to make notes on your actual progress, so you won't have to backtrack if you missed a step on one of the garments.

Don't try to streamline the pressing parts of garment construction. It does take a few extra minutes to press seams flat or turn under seam allowances, but you'll save time

TO IMPROVE YOUR SEWING, KEEP UP WITH NEW TIME- AND LABOR-SAVING TECHNIQUES.

have simply gotten used to in the past. And be sure to keep the tools and equipment that you already own in top working condition. Regular cleaning and maintenance of your sewing machine and serger will ensure many years of trouble-free stitching.

Speaking of your machines, it's a great idea to periodically reacquaint yourself with their stitching capabilities by re-reading the owner's manual. You will very likely learn something new every time you go through the manual. Even if you studied it cover to cover when you first got the machine, it's easy to forget about features that you use less frequently or perhaps have never used at all. Make up some practice samples of the various stitches and stitch variations, making notes about needle and bobbin tension, stitch length and width, and other technical details. Compiling the samples and notes into a ready-reference notebook may come in handy when you're looking for the perfect machine embroidery stitch for jacket cuffs or vest fronts.

Lifelong Learning

The accelerated pace of new technological developments means that there will always be faster and more efficient ways to help us accomplish our objectives. Don't make the mistake of assuming that something you learned years ago still represents the best approach. Keep your mind open to new possibilities. It may take some effort to learn a new way of doing something, but you will likely profit in the long run.

When you take a particular sewing class to learn a specific new technique, you will probably gather many other time-saving construction tips and strategies from your teacher and classmates. Before you forget these great

A Stitch in Time

When you finish sewing for the day, take a few moments to clean and reorganize your work area. You'll appreciate coming back to a workspace that is ready to go.

ideas, jot them down in your notebook for future reference and periodically review the notebook to see what you can try at home.

Pay special attention to the "Stitch in Time" and "Tips from the Designer" insets in this book. Look for other books and magazines devoted to helping you improve your sewing skills and efficiency. You can find terrific new books, magazines, and instructional videos at your local sewing center, bookstore, and library. Take a class or teach a class.

A WELL-FITTING GARMENT IS OBVIOUS, AND FLATTERING.

A Stitch in Time

Assembly-line principles applied to your sewing projects will speed up the construction process, allowing more time to spend on the decorative touches that show off your originality.

Contact your sewing store, your Extension Service, the community college, and local high school to investigate opportunities to teach what you already know. You'll be pleasantly surprised to find out how much you can learn from your students.

Idea Notebook:

CREATIVE COLLAR TREATMENTS

Turn simple style into sensational cachet by applying your creative ideas to collars, lapels, and necklines. A little pizzazz goes a long way to frame your face beautifully.

INTERESTING TEXTURED YARNS FROM YOUR LOCAL KNITTING OR WEAVING STORE CAN BE COUCHED TO THE SURFACE OF COLLAR AND LAPELS, FOR A TRULY UNIQUE LOOK. DESIGNER: MARY PARKER.

THREADS COUCHED TO THE COLLAR AND LAPELS IN A GEOMETRIC PATTERN ENHANCE THE LUSCIOUS COLORS OF THIS SILK TWEED JACKET. COUCHING WITH INVISIBLE NYLON THREAD ENSURES THAT THE THREAD COLORS STAY BRIGHT AND INTENSE. DESIGNER: MARY PARKER.

When you're experimenting with a technique, show off your best efforts on the collar, lapels, or neckline area of a jacket or vest. The area to be worked is small, so it doesn't require a lot of time. The result? You get to practice your skills, and the finished garment benefits from your creative innovation.

A SMALL BREAST POCKET ADDED TO A CLASSIC VEST MAKES PICTURE-PERFECT SPACE FOR A LACY HANKIE. A SURPRISING TOUCH THAT LOOKS RIGHT AT HOME. DESIGNER: JUDITH ROBERTSON.

THE SEMINOLE PATCH-WORK TRIM ON THIS BRIGHT AND BOLD FASHION HELPS DISTIN-GUISH THE COLLAR AND LAPELS FROM THE UNDERLYING JACKET BODY. THESE EMBELL-ISHED LAPELS WILL DRAMATICALLY FRAME A DEEP-TONED PURPLE OR INDIGO BLUE DRESS. DESIGNER: M. LUANNE CARSON.

NECKLINE INTEREST CAN BE ELEGANTLY SUBTLE, AS IN THIS CARDIGAN-STYLE JACKET. LEFTOVER FABRIC WAS UNRAVELED TO PROVIDE THE THREAD FOR THIS COUCHED DECORATION. DESIGNER: JUDITH ROBERTSON.

Two rows of soutache cord stitched to the surface visually narrow these wide lapels and add design interest at the same time. The whimsical ladybug buttons further distract the eye from the lapel width. Designer: Mary Parker.

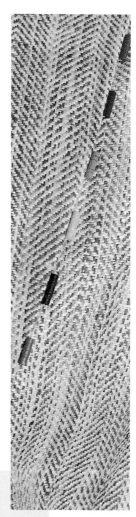

At first glance, the accents of color on this vest's lapels appear to be satin stitched, but upon closer examination turn out to be tubular wooden beads tacked to the edges. An open-minded approach to embellishment yields happy results. Designer: Judith Robertson.

Braid trim sewn to lapel edges and pocket welts adds a deluxe finish to a patterned fabric, and creates a bold linear accent. Designer: Mary Parker.

THE IRIDESCENT PIPING ALONG THIS JACKET'S FRONT AND NECKLINE OPENING SETS OFF THE RICH COLOR AND TEXTURE OF THE FABRIC. WITHOUT THIS ACCENT AND THE BREAST POCKET HANKIE, THE JACKET WOULD BE JUST ANOTHER COLLARLESS STYLE. DESIGNER: MARY PARKER.

THE COLLAR OF THIS VEST WAS MADE MORE INTERESTING BY CRINKLING THE CONTRASTING FABRIC AND ADDING ANTIQUE BUTTON ACCENTS. DESIGNER: MARY PARKER.

STRIPS OF THE TWEED FABRIC TOPSTITCHED TO THE UPPER COLLAR ADD GRAPHIC INTEREST TO THIS JACKET. THE TWEED STRIPS ALSO BLEND THE CONTRASTING COLLAR WITH THE REST OF THE GARMENT. DESIGNER: MARY PARKER.

A Stitch in Time

Be open-minded about new ideas and test-drive new products that may save time or improve your sewing technique.

FINISHING TOUCHES FOR FINISHING FLAIR

A new garment isn't truly done until you've imprinted it with your personal signature. The smallest detail that reflects the essence of your creativity can make a world of difference. It can transform an ordinary garment into a spectacular one and guarantee that it won't get pushed to the back of your closet. You may have already incorporated some unusual details during the construction process, such as contrast pocket welts, colorful double-piped edges, decorative topstitching, or a series of strategically-placed tucks and pleats. Perhaps you've used the construction process to show off some of your other needlework skills by making smocked or ruched inserts.

However, if you flew through construction, saving the embellishment until the end, you can still choose from a wide selection of fancy braids, cords, ribbons, tassels, laces, sequins, and tatted edgings for a decorative exclamation point. Or, a scattering of appliqués might be just the perfect accent for an otherwise ho-hum vest that you want to jazz up a bit. Don't be afraid to experiment with embroidery or other decorative stitching that you can add either by hand or by machine. And, for the truly patient, the application of beadwork can give your new garment a glittering look that can't be duplicated.

BUTTON UP

The creative use of buttons and other closures can often distinguish an otherwise plain garment. These fasteners can make the same garment look dressed-up, dressed-down, or anywhere in between. Buttons today come in a dizzying array of colors, shapes, sizes, and materials. Experiment with how they look on your new project, and use them to refresh your older garments, too. The most difficult part about button-shopping is realizing that you actu-

ally, finally, must make a decision about which single button or set of buttons to buy. Use buttons in unusual places on the garment, perhaps placing a few on the upper sleeve, on a pocket or along the front hem in a decorative arrangement. Draw attention to an otherwise plain collar with a small group of pearl buttons sewn into the collar-point area. Don't overlook the element of flair that you can achieve by using Chinese knotted loops and buttons, fabric button-loops, and other types of fabric closures made in complementary and contrasting colors. Look at the designer garments on pages 30-33 for some interesting and ingenious garment closures.

If you just can't come up with the perfect crowning touch for your new garment, turn to the wealth of ideas in your inspiration library and scan the photographs in this book. Once you inspire yourself with what other designers have devised, you will surely design your own unique perfect solution.

Opportunities for making a personal design statement abound, and it's up to you to take advantage of them and make them work for you. The finishing touches that you, and only you, add to your original fashions will reflect your creativity and personal cachet.

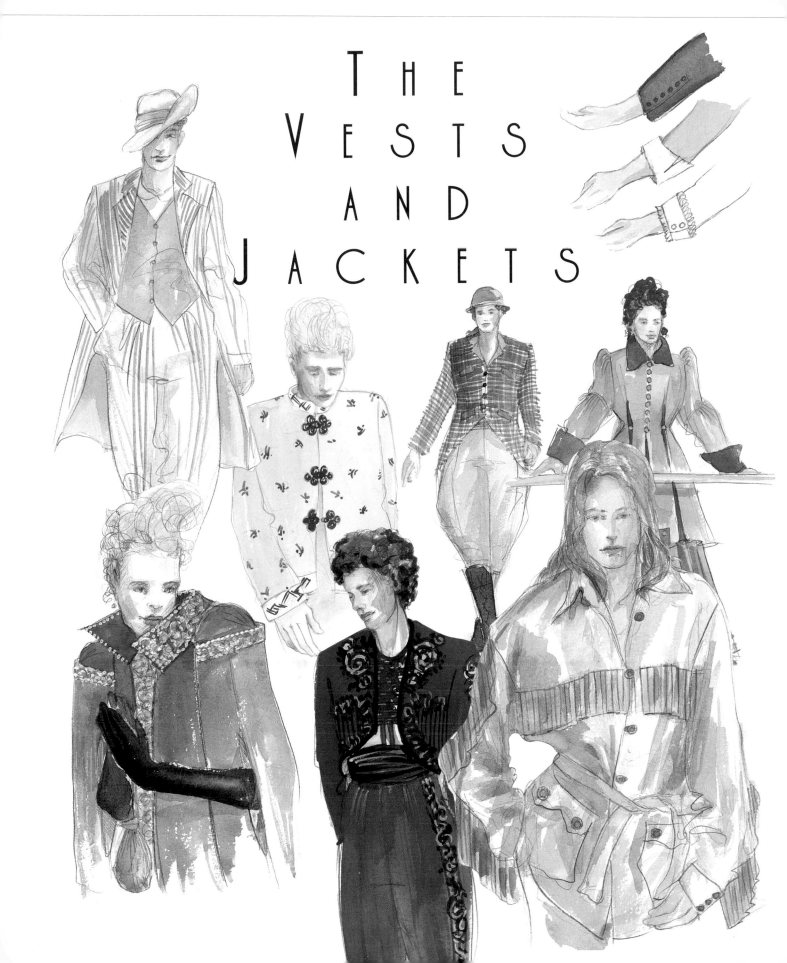

THE
VESTS
AND
JACKETS

Sheer Delight

DESIGNER
M. Luanne Carson

The stripes in this ultra-sheer light-as-air shirt jacket play off each other to create unique graphic interest and a sophisticated look.

Design and construction details

The designer chose a roomy overblouse pattern to give herself room to experiment with the different linear effects possible.

■ The interaction among the various stripe directions (horizontal, vertical, diagonal) engages the eye and makes this simple garment design truly spectacular. The sleeves are cut on the bias, to contrast with the grid of the blouse body. The pockets, collar, and back overlay provide right-angle contrast to the layers below, for a dimensional quality not possible in a simple plaid.

■ The designer used self-fabric bias binding to finish raw edges and cover construction features. The bias direction of the binding adds a nice counterpoint to the regularity of the grid design.

Tips from the designer

■ Take advantage of the time- and labor-saving devices that are available today. I made more than 8 yards (7.35 m) of self-fabric bias binding for this jacket, and was extremely thankful for the bias tape maker!

Galaxy's End
DESIGNER
Pat Scheible

Discover the sparkling gems in your collection of fabrics and trims, and use them to transform an earthly jacket pattern into an extraterrestrial marvel.

Design details

The designer made a Japanese-inspired jacket according to pattern directions, without any alterations. However, she reached for the stars when it came to inventive use of fabric and embellishment.

■ The unusual shapes of many ethnic pattern components lend themselves to individual interpretation. The asymmetrical front panels, connecting belt, and shaped hemline of this jacket defy conventional treatment. The designer made beautiful use of these areas to showcase unique fabrics and have fun with purely decorative touches.

■ Because she had more of the ikat fabric than anything else, she used it as the foundation for the entire jacket, playing off its colors and pattern with the planetary print. However, the planets fabric was too bright next to the ikat, so she used its wrong side and toned it down with an overlay of black chiffon. The hazy, dimensional effect created by the chiffon was a welcome surprise.

■ She machine quilted the layers together with free-form stitching in an iridescent blue silk thread. The planets fabric inspired a stitch design reminiscent of radio signals from deep space.

■ Inspired by the fabrics, she continued her creative voyage with a sprinkling of star-shaped sequins, glowing planets, and sun/moon buttons.

■ To balance the complexity of the front panel, she chose a tranquil midnight blue for the adjoining sleeve and added unifying bands of black chiffon at both cuffs.

"I adore fabrics, but am a miser. I never can bring myself to buy enough of one exquisite thing to complete a pattern. To conjure up an attractive garment from bits and pieces forces me to think creatively, and makes each project a victory."

Harmonic Convergence

DESIGNER
M. Luanne Carson

The most unique designs, such as this vest, often result from the coming together of unexpected and unplanned elements.

The chain was put into service as a front fastener, held in place by a looped strip of suede. A single link turned up in the custom lapel embellishment, which also includes a button, bead, horn tube, and strip of suede. The fabric folds at the front hem were a spur of the moment experiment, which turned out to be a very special and individualized finishing touch.

Tips from the designer

■ Save everything! The smallest bits and scraps can provide the perfect touch to your creative efforts. For example, the tortoise shell chain was expensive, so I bought just a little bit and found a way to work it into this vest. Even a single link turned out to be a great contribution to the lapel "pin."

■ Listen to your inner voice, especially when it tells you that a project still needs "something" to be complete. Set the piece aside and let your creative mind work on it for a while. The perfect solution might be triggered by a photograph, a button, a garment you see passing by, or simply by experimenting with different options until they converge into the "right" answer.

Design details

The designer varied a pattern for a Japanese-inspired vest by using the reverse side of the fabric for contrasting lapels. However, when she finished making the vest, she felt it still didn't look complete. Months later, she pulled it from her collection of garments awaiting a final touch of inspiration and began to play around with a length of just-purchased faux tortoise shell chain.

Prairie Point Style
D E S I G N E R
Barbara Fugazzotto

The natural sheen of these silk fabrics and the modified prairie points in a geometric arrangement create a sleek architectural effect.

Design and construction details

The designer started with a standard pattern for a dartless vest and made it special with custom-pieced yardage, several carefully placed prairie points, and a few decorative buttons.

■ She first cut the pattern out of a muslin foundation fabric and stitched the pieced bands of two silks to the muslin.

■ She incorporated some modified prairie points into some of the pieced seams (see illustration), limiting the number of points to avoid "design overkill."

■ Because this vest is meant to be worn open, she used some perfectly coordinating buttons for their decorative value, instead of creating a functional button/buttonhole arrangement.

Tips from the designer

■ The two silk fabrics were next to each other on my fabric shelves and, at first glance, seemed to clash with one another. But it struck me that this clashing quality could be energizing to a garment design. I think the result shows how careful strip piecing of two opposing colors can harmonize them into an elegant fashion.

■ I like these modified prairie points because they expose three fabric surfaces, which is very interesting with shiny fabrics. The light hits the three surfaces in different ways and creates intriguing shadows. Striped fabrics give a completely different, but equally interesting, effect.

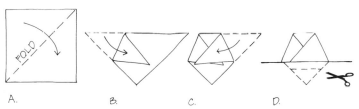

A.   B.   C.   D.

Figure 1: To make modified prairie points, cut a square of fabric to desired size. Fold in half diagonally (A). Fold left point over to meet opposite edge (B). Fold right point over to meet opposite edge (C). Stitch folded point into seam and trim excess from seam allowance (D).

Hearts Aglow
DESIGNER
M. Luanne Carson

Heart-printed sleeves coupled with a quilted burgundy silk combine to make a luscious jacket that projects a warming glow.

■ She echoed the diagonal lines of the quilted silk in the angled front opening and the V-shaped lines of the pocket and top button closure. The "windows" created behind the pocket opening and button closure were filled with luminous coordinating silk to create a glowing stained glass effect. The golden highlights of the heart-printed silk provide random glimmers of light along the piping.

■ For variety from front to back, she used different buttons to coordinate with their immediate surroundings and act as interesting focal points. Another contrast: the buttons on the front are contemporary, while those on the back are antique.

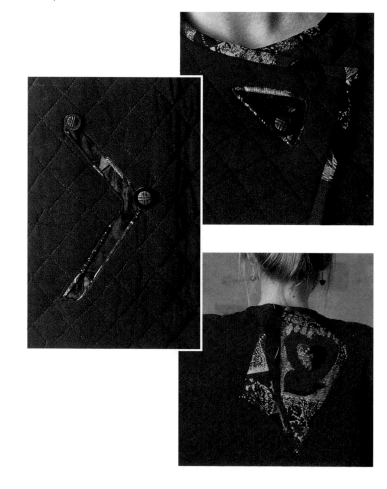

Design and construction details

The designer experimented with contrasts in this jacket by combining feather-weight fabrics with rich, dark colors and a quilted effect to suggest hefty warmth, and by setting angular shapes against a soft, contoured ground.

Felted Wool Wonder

DESIGNER
Elma Johnson

Make your own version of a boiled wool jacket by felting machine-knitted yardage in the washing machine and then sewing up a warm and wonderful fashion.

Design details

The designer, an accomplished textile artist, has been experimenting with a knitting machine and wanted to do something special with the lengths of knit yardage that are so quick and easy to produce. She felted the knitted wool by machine-washing it in the hottest water possible and then stretching it on a homemade frame. The finished fabric is unbelievably thick and luscious, doesn't ravel, and makes a very warm and soft garment.

Construction details

To knit the yardage:

1. Use medium-weight (3- to 6-ply) wool yarn and a knitting machine that can handle the selected yarn weight. The designer used about 4 pounds (9 kilograms) of rug yarn.

2. Start knitting with scrap yarn for 6" (15 cm) or more. The extra scrap yarn on each end of the yardage will come in handy when stretching the felted fabric, because it takes the stress off the fashion fabric and enables you to use every inch of the intended yardage for your garment.

3. Knit all of the selected yarn, as wide as possible and using all needles on the knitting machine bed. At intervals of 12-18" (30.5-45.5 cm), knit or tie a piece of contrasting colored yarn or string to each edge; these "markers" will help you keep the fabric's grain straight when stretching.

4. Depending on the yarn, you will end up with about 7-8 yards (6.4-7.4 m) of knitted fabric. At this point, it will not be very attractive, but the felting will condense everything nicely. See Designer Tip below about estimating shrinkage.

5. With scrap yarn, knit 6" (16 cm) or more, and bind off. Do not remove scrap ends until fabric has been felted, stretched, and completely dried.

To felt the yardage:

1. Fill washing machine with the hottest possible water to a level that just covers the knitted yardage.

2. While machine is filling, add ¼ cup (35 g) liquid or powder detergent, and set machine on wash cycle.

3. Prop the lid open so that machine will not begin the spin cycle, which will produce more lint than any washing machine can handle. Also, you will probably felt, or wash, the yardage more than once to get the desired effect.

4. At the end of the wash cycle, stop the machine and examine the fabric by squeezing the water out of a small area. Decide whether you want the fabric to be felted more; if so, reset the machine and repeat the wash cycle. It is not necessary to add more hot water or detergent.

5. When the fabric has felted to your satisfaction, stop the machine.

6. Using a pitcher and big buckets, dip out the water from the washing machine, taking every precaution to keep lint from going down (and clogging) the drain. The designer used a series of buckets with kitchen strainers lined with elastic-ended paint strainer bags (available at paint stores), and a sink drain strainer cut to size from a pot scrubber pad. As she dipped and poured water first into the buckets and strainers, and finally into a strainer in the sink, different fiber lengths were caught at each screen. Remove as much water as possible, and dispose of fibers and lint left behind in strainers.

7. Refill the washing machine with cold water, add fabric softener, and run through the wash cycle again.

8. Repeat the water-dipping procedure. Wring out as much water from the fabric as possible and transfer fabric to sink to drain.

9. Let felted fabric drain for an hour or so, but do not let it dry.

For the stretcher frame:

The size of the stretcher frame will be determined by the length of the fabric. The knitted fabric will shrink about 30 percent, but will vary with the type of yarn and the number of times it is washed (see Designer Tip below).

1. Estimate the shrinkage of your felted fabric.

2. Using 1" x 3" (2.5 x 7.5 cm) lumber, make a rectangular frame as long as your fabric and as wide as your felted yardage will stretch. The designer's knitting machine bed is 39" (99 cm) wide; however, the yardage draws in as a result of the knitting process and even more from the felting. She built her stretcher frame 30" (76 cm) wide, because that is the widest the felted fabric will stretch. For convenient handling and storage, make two or three frames that attach to one another lengthwise; however, handle as one frame when stretching the fabric and use only the four outside bars. Construct frame with sturdy corner bolts or braces. See illustration.

3. Mark dots along all four sides of frame, 1" (2.5 cm) apart, keeping them in an even line and opposite one another.

4. Drill holes through the frame at each dot.

5. Using aluminum or galvanized nails that are 1½" (4 cm) long and a little bigger around than the drilled holes, drive a nail through each hole from the back side so ½" (1.25 cm) protrudes on the front side.

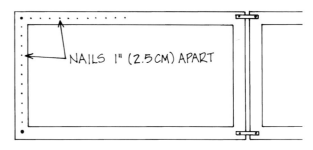

NAILS 1" (2.5 CM) APART

JOINING STRETCHER FRAMES

To stretch the felted fabric:

The fabric must be stretched slowly and firmly across the entire frame's length and width. Do not try to stretch the fabric from nail to adjacent nail, which will stress the fabric and may stretch it off grain.

1. Hook top left corner of the felted fabric on the top left nail of the frame. Hook the top right fabric corner on the top right nail. Repeat with bottom left and right corners.

2. Hook the midpoint of the fabric's top edge on the middle nail of the frame's top bar; repeat at bottom.

3. Hook the midpoint of the fabric's left edge to the middle nail of the frame's left edge; repeat on the right edge.

4. Continue finding the midpoints on the top, bottom, and side edges of the frame, gently stretching and hooking the fabric to corresponding nails as you go. Use pliers to help you grip and stretch the fabric; this process can be hard on the hands.

5. Make sure the contrasting color markers along the edges of the fabric remain opposite one another, to preserve the fabric's straight grain.

6. Let fabric dry completely on the frame.

7. Remove from frame and brush fabric surface with a brass wire brush to remove more lint, small burrs, and other small debris from the yarn. Steam press fabric or use as is.

Tips from the designer

■ The extra work to dip the water out with buckets and strainers is worth it, because you won't have to call the plumber to unclog the drain when you're through. You will also notice that different types and lengths of fiber lint will be caught at each strainer.

■ To estimate how much a fabric will shrink when felted, it's critical that you make some samples. Knit several 12" (30.5 cm) samples of your selected yarn. Alternatively, knit some samples of any length and attach markers 12" (30.5 cm) apart. Run the samples through the felting process, smooth out, let dry, and measure. If the 12" (30.5 cm) length now measures 8" (20.5 cm), or two-thirds of the original length, the shrinkage is 33 percent. For each 1 yard (.95 m) of finished fabric that you want, you will have to knit 33 percent more, or 1⅓ yards (1.2 m).

■ After the fabric has finished felting, don't let it dry before stretching it. Trying to re-wet it and stretch it later is terribly hard on you and the yarn.

■ When constructing a garment with this thick felted wool, it's best to bind hem and opening edges to cut down on bulk. For interior construction, use a lot of steam when pressing seams open or butt raw edges together and cover seam with braid or other trim.

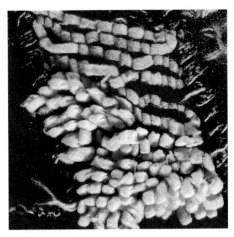

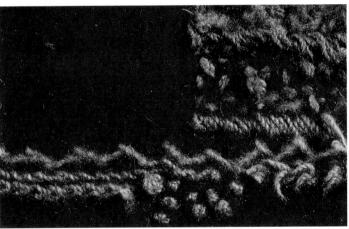

DIFFERENT TYPES OF YARNS AND YARN COMBINATIONS RESULT IN EXCITINGLY VARIED FELTED FABRICS. MULTICOLORED YARNS AND BOUCLÉ OR OTHER TEXTURED YARNS, SUCH AS THOSE SHOWN HERE, CAN PRODUCE BEAUTIFUL SURPRISES.

BEFORE FELTING, THE KNIT FABRIC IS SCRAWNY LOOKING AND NOT TERRIBLY ATTRACTIVE. AFTER FELTING, THE FIBERS CONSOLIDATE AND THE FABRIC GETS THICK AND LUSCIOUSLY SOFT.

The beautiful silk prints of these recycled men's neckties combine to make a truly unique vest collar, especially when topped off with assorted buttons and baubles.

Materials and supplies

- Pattern for collarless vest
- Fashion fabric and lining, as required by pattern
- Assorted neckties, at least five or six
- Permanent press muslin, ¼ yard (.25 m)
- Tracing or pattern-making paper and pencil
- Notions required by pattern

Design and construction details

1. Hand wash ties in mild soap, squeezing rather than twisting them. Rinse well and hang to dry.

2. Open ties up, remove interfacing, and press flat.

3. Cut vest fronts and back from fashion fabric and lining; set aside.

4. To draft the collar pattern, trace the vest front pattern piece along the cutting lines. Select a shoulder point about midway between neck and armhole at point A (see Figure 1). Make a mark at the break point of the vest's front edge (point B). Draw a line from point C at the midpoint of the bottom edge to point B. Draw a line from point A to B-C and make a mark at intersection point D. Add seam allowances to A-D and B-D. Cut out collar pattern.

5. To design the patchwork arrangement of necktie pieces, make two mirror-image copies of the collar pattern. With a pencil, divide the collar pattern into smaller segments that combine to make a pleasing appearance. See Figure 2 for the designer's arrangement of tie blocks J, K, L, M, N, O, and P; the dotted lines indicate how the ties were pieced together in blocks and then joined to make the collar; the numbers indicate the sewing sequence of each block of ties.

6. Cut collar pattern out of muslin; cut ties according to the areas of your patchwork design.

7. Beginning with block J, sew a tie piece to the muslin base at the shoulder line. Use ¼" (6 mm) seams for all patchwork and press seams as you go.

8. Sew block K together in a long strip.

9. Add block L to block K.

10. Add block K-L to block J by placing them right sides together and sewing a ¼" (6 mm) seam directly to the muslin base.

11. Press collar flat and trim any uneven areas to match the muslin base.

12. Repeat for blocks M, N, O, P.

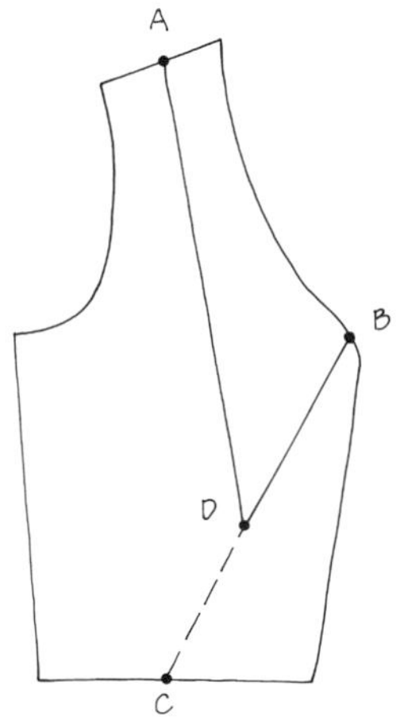

FIG.1

DRAFTING COLLAR PATTERN

13. Right sides together, line the pieced collars, leaving shoulder seams open. Trim seams, turn through the shoulders, and press.

14. Assemble vest according to pattern instructions, stitching collars into shoulder seam.

15. Overlap the two collars at center front and hand-tack in place. Embellish finished collar and vest as desired.

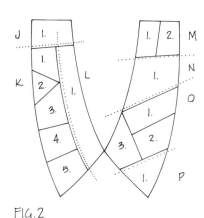

FIG.2

ASSEMBLING PATCHWORK COLLAR

Tips from the designer

■ Don't be surprised if several of the ties bleed color when you wash them. However, I have found that they don't seem to stain one another.

■ When designing your collar, be creative with lines A-D and B-D; they could be curved, scalloped, shorter, or longer.

■ Embellishment options are numerous! Think about couching decorative yarns along the patchwork lines before lining the collars, or add some silk ribbon embroidery, beadwork, or lace.

■ Instead of putting buttonholes in the vest, wear it open and use buttons for their decorative, rather than functional, value.

Plan for the Week

Monday

Tuesday
Pretreat ties and fabrics.

Wednesday
Open ties, remove interfacing, and press; cut out vest fronts and backs.

Thursday
Design collar pattern; cut out tie pieces.

Friday
Piece collar blocks and sew to muslin base.

Saturday
Line collars; begin vest construction.

Sunday
Complete vest construction; attach embellishments.

East Meets West

DESIGNER

Aileen S. Gugenheim

Create a beautiful melting pot of fabrics in this kimono-inspired jacket. with Japanese Kasuri fabrics and very Western denim prints.

Design and construction details

The designer combined the asymmetrical features of a kimono-style jacket pattern with the good fit of a basic Western-style jacket pattern. By comparing the kimono pattern pieces with the well-fitting jacket pieces, she was able to refine the fit of the finished garment before cutting into the sumptuous fabrics and beginning the elaborate design work.

■ She made a quick muslin of the Western-style jacket pattern to check the sleeve width and armhole ease required for comfortable wear. She, therefore, knew in advance what alterations the kimono pattern would require for good fit. This is especially important for kimono patterns that call for slight padding, which may restrict movement in the armhole and shoulder area if additional ease is not figured in.

■ While the designer likes the asymmetrical lines of the kimono, she feels that the usual dropped shoulder is unflattering to many body types. She, therefore, changed the shoulder line according to her jacket muslin. This gave her a flattering fit, without compromising the interest of an asymmetrical kimono front.

■ She also prefers the well-fitting two-piece sleeve of the basic jacket pattern to the straight-cut one-piece kimono sleeve. By substituting sleeve styles, she achieved better fit and was able to easily add width in the upper arm area for wearing comfort.

■ She placed the specialty fabric (the Japanese Kasuri floral print) at the top of the garment, framing the face. This is where observers look first, so it's the best position for the most important design elements.

■ Assorted coordinating fabrics were chosen for design interest and their ability to enhance the overall look of the garment. Small prints and stripes result in interesting visual effects when cut on the bias for the decorative strips.

■ The designer used tailor's chalk to draw the meandering pathways for the bias strips; she chalked right on the cut-out pattern pieces and brushed off the excess later on. Where the bias strips cross from one pattern piece to another, she made a small clip in the side or shoulder seam allowances of both pieces, to mark the place where the strips must connect.

■ After the bias strips were attached, she evaluated the garment pieces for additional design options, from appliqué shapes to unusual buttons, lines of zigzag stitching to couched threads.

■ She lined the garment in silk, because it slips on easier than other fabrics. And she built a "secret" pocket into the lining, because pockets in the outer fashion fabric can bulge out and disrupt the smooth line of the garment.

■ Because of its layered construction, the finished garment can be quite weighty. To make sure the hem hangs properly, with enough heft to balance the rest of the garment, she cut bias strips from muslin or sheeting fabric and used them as hem facings.

Tips from the designer

■ It seems to take more time to plan your design than actually sew it, so you might want to play around with paper design elements before you actually cut into your valuable fabrics. Also, arranging and rearranging cut-out shapes can be a lot less intimidating than sketching or drawing.

■ When you lavish this much attention on a gorgeous original fashion, don't skimp on the button. Look for a wonderful, showy closure that also relates to the theme of the entire garment.

"I like to 'draw' with the
bias strips, as an artist
does on a canvas.
This technique helps me
look at the whole garment as
a unified design."

Polar Poppies
DESIGNER
Karen M. Bennett

For a fresh new look, use a traditional appliqué technique with a modern fabric like fleece.

Materials and supplies

- Pattern for a short collarless jacket
- 1½ yard (1.4 m) fleece for body of jacket
- ⅛ yard (.15 m) contrasting fleece for appliqué poppy shapes
- 1/8 yard (.15 m) contrasting fleece for trim
- Nylon sewing thread
- Water-soluble stabilizer
- Fray retardant
- Ballpoint sewing machine needle
- Buttons and notions, as required by pattern

Construction details

1. Cut out jacket pattern pieces, according to pattern's cutting layout.

2. Cut poppy shapes, or other desired appliqué shapes, out of contrasting fleece.

3. Cut out two strips of contrasting trim along the crosswise grain, ¼" (6 mm) wide. Gently pull on each end, so the edges will curl to the wrong side.

4. Turn sleeve hem under and baste in place, with nylon thread in the needle and regular thread in the bobbin. Use a long basting stitch.

5. Position poppy or other appliqué shape on right side of sleeve, with bottom point just touching the basting line. Pin in place.

6. Using a long zigzag, stitch trimming strip over basting line, just catching the edge of the trim. When you reach the appliqué shape, butt the trimming strip to it and stitch around the appliqué with the sewing machine foot centered over the line where the appliqué and trim meet. You may need to shorten the stitch as you go around the curves. Repeat on other sleeve.

7. Sew the underarm seam, shoulder seams, side seams, and insert sleeves.

8. Turn under hem on bottom, neckline, and front opening edges; machine baste as above.

9. Beginning at a side seam, apply trim and appliqué shapes as above.

10. Make buttonholes (see designer tip below) and attach buttons.

Tips from the designer

- Fleece has a tendency to stretch and warp along the crosswise grain at the edges. Therefore, when planning your designs, try to avoid intricate sewing along the edges of the appliqué shapes.

- Do not iron fleece. It will show the slightest touch of the iron and may melt the fibers. This is from the voice of experience!

- Be very careful when making buttonholes, and use plenty of stabilizer (I placed four layers on top and four on the bottom). Make the buttonholes through the layers of stabilizer and then wash them away completely. Apply fray retardant to the back of the buttonholes and let dry completely before cutting open.

- When attaching buttons, a small button on the wrong side adds needed support.

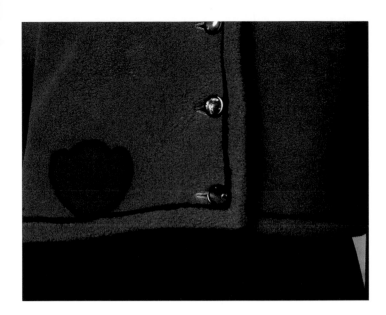

Plan for the Week

Monday

~~~

Tuesday

~~~

Wednesday
Lay out, cut, and mark jacket pattern.

Thursday
Cut out appliqué shapes and trimming strips.

Friday
Attach trim and appliqué shapes to sleeves; begin jacket construction.

Saturday
Complete jacket construction; attach trim and appliqué shapes to hem, neckline, and front opening edges.

Sunday
Mark and make buttonholes; mark and attach buttons.

"Living in a 1930s cottage inspired me to experiment with designs from the Arts and Crafts movement, such as the poppy."

Cranberry Disguise

DESIGNER
M. Luanne Carson

You'd never guess that this fabulous fashion was made from scraps of flawed double knit. It's proof that creativity can overcome any challenge.

Design and construction details

The designer made two capes from this double knit fabric and wanted to eke out as many garments as possible from the original yardage. However, the leftover scraps had serious knitting flaws, which required careful placement of pattern pieces and ingenious embellishment.

■ She positioned the fabric flaws across from each other so the "cover-ups" would relate to one another across the front opening. The decorative assemblages are composed of assorted textures, braids, a sheer, and a puffed strip of print. The left side is accented with a decorative button, which also serves as the jumping off point for the self-fabric tube.

■ Because the designer particularly likes asymmetry, she let the fabric tube meander at random and yet connect the two vest fronts literally and figuratively. The free-hanging button dangle and curved path of the tube helps loosen up the feel of the highly-structured fabric embellishments.

Tips from the designer

■ Don't get in a rut of thinking buttons are only for closures. They make wonderful design elements and don't have to function at all, except in a decorative sense. Simply hide the functional closures. In this vest, the actual fastener is a nylon snap beneath the fabric tube's knot.

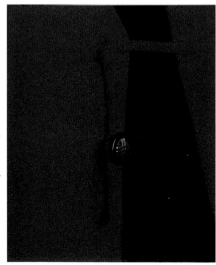

Three interesting looks were created by puffing or gathering alternate strips in this chevron design. One of these vests was a mistake. but you'd never know it!

Design and construction details

The designer started with a basic vest pattern and pieced the fronts with 3" (7.5 cm) strips, alternating between flat and "puffed," an heirloom sewing term for gathering.

■ The puffed strips can be smoothly gathered on a serger with differential feed, or on a regular sewing machine by drawing up rows of long stitches.

■ The designer cut the vest fronts out of a base fabric (muslin or flannel works well) and marked a 45-degree line on each one, in a mirror image and at the same position on each front. She positioned a puffed strip right side up on top of the base fabric and a flat strip on top of the puffed, right sides together, and stitched a ¼" (6 mm) seam through all three thicknesses. She then flipped the flat strip back down against the base fabric, finger pressed it, and placed the next puffed strip on top of the flat, right sides together, and stitched a seam as above. She continued until the base was covered and then trimmed excess strip fabric around the edges of the fronts. The vest was then constructed and lined as usual, substituting button loops for buttonholes.

Tips from the designer

■ Some fabrics gather better than others. I had trouble with the metallic silk fabric, but found that cotton fabric works beautifully.

■ This technique of mixing and puffing fabrics is great for experimenting with color, pattern, and texture. However, things don't always come out the way you had in mind, so be ready to improvise solutions. For example, the black fabric in the turquoise/black vest didn't lay flat, so I stipple quilted it. The metallic silk vest was a mistake, but you wouldn't know it; I accidentally made two left sides instead of a left and a right. To cover my error, I recut a solid right side and now it looks as if I planned the vest that way!

Turkish Mosaic

DESIGNER

Pat Scheible

A simple pattern based on rectangles can look dramatically different when highlighted with patterned ribbon trim, metallic thread and a stencil-like appliqué.

Design and construction details

The designer selected an easy-sew Turkish coat pattern composed of rectangles and straight seams. The contrasting borders and coat lining offer opportunities for creative fabric combinations.

■ She trimmed the dividing lines between contrasting panels with an intricately patterned ribbon and a subtle, but glittering, line of zigzag topstitching in metallic thread.

■ She attached the appliqué to the back before assembling the coat. Starting with a stencil-like design, she enlarged and transferred it to the back of the appliqué fabric. She then cut out the motifs one at a time and fused them to the coat.

Tips from the designer

■ There are so many design sources for this type of appliqué, from stencil patterns and Middle Eastern mosaic designs to calligraphy symbols and floral shapes. Have fun and explore.

■ When transferring designs for appliqué, take care that the motifs are pointing in the right direction before fusing on the backing. You don't want to end up with two right-facing motifs if you were aiming for a mirror image.

■ The lining fabric on a coat like this one can make a dramatic contrast to the outer fabric. Why choose a solid when you can offer a glimpse of a sumptuous pattern?

Gi, What A Jacket

DESIGNER

Joyce Baldwin

Inspiration for creative garments can come from anywhere. This attractive kimono-style jacket is based on the "gi," the white jacket worn by practitioners of karate.

Materials and supplies

- Pattern for kimono-style jacket, or pattern drafted from gi uniform

- Medium-weight fabric of choice for body of jacket

- Coordinating fabric for front band and belt

- Assorted fabrics for appliqué; the design shown here uses three different fabrics

- Lightweight fleece interfacing for front band and belt

- Notions required by pattern

Construction details

1. Draw design for appliqué or adapt appliqué motif from Oriental-inspired design. Enlarge appliqué design on photocopier.

2. Divide design into three sections and make individual pattern pieces. Cut pattern pieces from three assorted fabrics.

3. Determine position of appliqué design on jacket back and attach by hand or machine. If attaching by hand, allow ¼" (6 mm) seam allowances around all sides of each pattern piece; press under seam allowance before stitching to jacket back.

4. Assemble jacket according to pattern instructions. Interface front band with lightweight fleece and topstitch band in multiple rows, as desired.

5. For ties, cut four fabric strips 1¼" by 11" (3 by 28 cm). Press under one short end; press under ¼" (6 mm) along each long edge; fold strip in half lengthwise and press. Topstitch closed to pressed edges. Stitch unfinished short ends to inside of jacket (see illustration).

6. For belt, cut fleece interfacing and fabric strip 4" (10 cm) wide and 2¾ yards (2.55 m) long; baste interfacing to wrong side. Fold in half lengthwise, right sides together; stitch long edge and one short end in ¼" (6 mm) seam allowance. Turn belt right side out, fold in seam allowance on unfinished short end, and press. Topstitch belt in multiple rows, as desired.

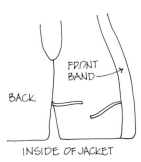

BACK

FRONT
BAND

INSIDE OF JACKET

7. To fasten jacket, bring one tie at interior band to tie at side slit on opposite side front and make bow. Lap loose front over other side and fasten remaining ties in same manner.

8. To fasten belt, position midpoint at center front of body; pass ends around body and back to center front, and tie.

Tips from the designer

■ This jacket makes a perfect showcase for your custom appliqué design. Draw your own or visit your local library or bookstore for books of copyright-free designs.

■ If you can't find a pattern for the fashion you have in mind, think about making your own from an already-finished garment. For more information, see *Patterns from Finished Clothes*, by Tracy Doyle (Sterling/Lark).

Plan for the Week

Monday

Tuesday

Begin sketches for appliqué motif or scan design books for motifs you can adapt.

Wednesday

Pretreat fabrics; complete sketch or enlargements of appliqué design.

Thursday

Lay out, cut, and mark jacket; interface appropriate pieces; cut out appliqué components.

Friday

Attach appliqué design; begin jacket construction.

Saturday

Complete jacket construction.

Sunday

Make and attach ties; make belt.

Tennessee Iris
DESIGNER
Judith S. Plucker

The state flower of Tennessee comes to life in this beautiful jacket that is lovingly assembled petal by petal, leaf by leaf.

Design and construction details

The designer started with a pattern for a simple dropped shoulder jacket and carefully assembled the custom fabric and appliqués. She designed the jacket to promote and benefit the first annual Iris Festival in Greeneville, Tennessee, and she wore it to every festival-related event.

■ She took her time when selecting the cotton fabrics for this garment: a hand-dyed background fabric similar to the designer's watercolor paintings, two purple prints that resemble iris petals, a green marbleized pattern, and a leaf pattern touched with gold.

■ She then collected bits of ribbon, metallic thread, and decorative yarns that might work with the jacket collage as it evolved.

■ Starting with the right front, she sketched ideas for the jacket's design on tracing paper, and then refined the first sketches on additional layers of tracing paper.

■ When the major design areas were finalized, she fused backing onto the selected fabrics, cut out appliqué shapes according to her design, and satin stitched them onto a muslin jacket foundation. For a three-dimensional effect, she cut some flower petals larger than needed, to allow for crimping and wrinkling.

■ She then filled the areas between the major design elements with Seminole patchwork, textured fabric, cording and ribbon trim, and additional appliqué until the entire muslin foundation was covered.

■ Finally, the jacket was assembled, lined, and finished with cotton bias binding.

CRIMPING THE FABRIC ADDS DEPTH AND TEXTURE TO THE SURFACE OF THE JACKET, AND THE METALLIC SATIN STITCHING ECHOES THE GOLD-ACCENTED LEAF PRINT.

Tips from the designer

■ When you're choosing fabrics for a garment composition, try to allow plenty of time. Make sure you've seen and considered many possibilities. And don't be afraid of buying more than you need for any one project. Your design may change as you work on the piece, and your fabric needs will change right along with it. Any scraps or unused pieces can always find a home in other projects.

■ Don't be tempted to make do and substitute a different fabric or trim for what you originally intended; it will always bother you. On the other hand, be open to surprising combinations you didn't envision beforehand.

RIGHT: WRINKLING THE FABRIC BEFORE FUSING IT TO A BACKING RESULTS IN AN INTERESTING THREE-DIMENSIONAL EFFECT, JUST RIGHT FOR TEXTURED FLOWER PETALS.

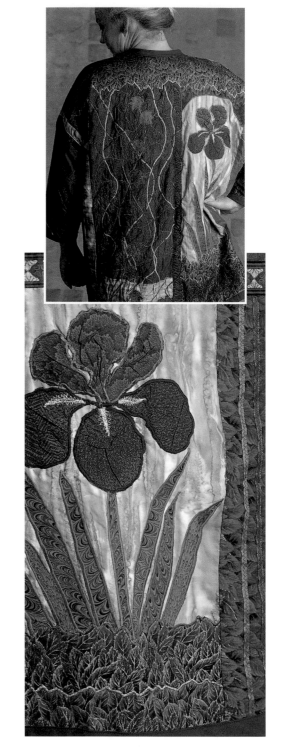

"I approached this jacket design as if I were painting with fabrics instead of watercolors, and it has become one of my favorite pieces of wearable art."

A Hands-Down Success

DESIGNER
Beth Karjala

Give a store-bought jacket a new life or look with appliqués cut from interesting fabrics.

Materials and supplies

- Ready-to-wear or completed jacket of choice

- ½ yard (.5 m) accent fabric with a bold design

- Matching thread and metallic or rayon embroidery thread for topstitching

- Fusible stabilizer

- Single and double/twin sewing machine needles

Design and construction details

The designer started with a ready-to-wear jacket made from an interesting silk fabric. She stitched on appliqués of hands from a boldly patterned African cloth to add interest and create an easy, but unique, fashion original.

- She fused a stabilizer to the wrong side of the African fabric and cut out the desired appliqué shapes. In the jacket shown here, the hand designs are 4" x 6" (10 x 15 cm) ovals.

- She then arranged the ovals on the jacket to get a satisfying overall design, and topstitched them in place with a contrasting thread color to highlight the patterns.

- For a finishing touch, she used the same contrasting thread in a double needle to create trapunto patterns on the background silk.

- To add a convenient pocket to the jacket front, the designer overlapped three design ovals, stitched along the overlapped lines, and then attached the trio to the garment, leaving the top edge open as the pocket opening.

Tips from the designer

- If you are adding a boldly contrasting color to the finished garment, provide some visual transition to the background fabric. For example, stitch designs into the background with contrasting or metallic thread to blend the background and appliquéd design elements.

- Stitching around design shapes with a double or twin needle gives a three-dimensional trapunto effect, in a fraction of the time it takes to do real trapunto. And leaving the thread tails hanging gives a nice wispy dimension.

Pattern Language

DESIGNER
M. Luanne Carson

Fabrics by themselves can be the source of innovative design. The intriguing pattern of this simple vest seems to display a hieroglyphic code all its own.

Design and construction details

The designer selected a vest pattern with few construction features, so it wouldn't detract from the engaging design of the cloth. For the same reason, she used embellishment sparingly.

■ She took advantage of the fabric's loose weave and unraveled threads for a self-fabric fringe. This is also a sure way to find a trim that matches the fabric perfectly.

■ She redesigned the back vent and added a decorative button, to create an unexpected detail to the back.

Tips from the designer

■ When a fabric has enough interest in itself, don't drown it with decoration. Let it speak for itself and add a few simple, yet creative, touches to make it sing.

■ If the fabric you choose has repeating motifs, like this one, do try to coordinate design elements at noticeable areas such as the front opening or back seam. Don't forget that you might need just a little extra material for such matching.

Designer Fashion
DESIGNER
Elizabeth Searle

A classic vest dons a new identity with a display of designer labels that also adds decorative bits of color.

Design and construction details

The designer made a basic vest pattern out of linen and collected assorted garment labels to use as the decorative emphasis.

■ She backed the labels with fusible stabilizer and then fused them to the vest fronts before assembling the vest, avoiding the buttonhole and front overlap areas. To hold everything safely in place, she covered the vest fronts with bridal hem binding, which is a nearly invisible net-like fabric, and then stitched around each label through all layers. When the vest is completed, the lining hides all the stitching on the inside.

■ For the custom covered buttons, the designer layered vest fabric, garment label, and bridal netting.

Tips from the designer

■ If you sew most of your own clothes, like I do, you won't have a lot of garment labels in your wardrobe. So collect them from your kids' clothes or invite your friends and family to donate labels to the vest cause.

■ When attached, the labels add some bulk to the fronts, so it's a good idea to interface the vest fabric or add a layer of lightweight flannel between the fabric and lining, to add some stability to the finished garment.

■ I'm a dressmaker and have labels of my own (Elizabeth Helene) to sew into the garments I make for my clients. I made sure my own labels are on this vest, along with the "big names."

Marbled Earthscape
DESIGNER
Mary S. Parker

Use your practice pieces from a fabric-marbling class to create a beautiful custom yardage that makes a truly unique vest.

Materials and supplies

■ Vest pattern of choice, preferably one that finishes all edges with binding

■ Assorted pieces of marbled silk fabric

■ Lining fabric, as required by pattern

■ Purchased bias binding, or coordinating fabric of choice to make custom bias binding

■ Rotary cutter and mat, or cutting supplies

■ Notions required by pattern

Construction details

1. Using a rotary cutter for speed, cut the marbled silk into lengthwise strips, in widths of your choice. Cut strips along crosswise grain into pieces sized as desired. Set scraps aside, to fill in small areas later.

2. Reassemble the lengthwise strips from the assorted marbled pieces. Stitch along the crosswise grain and press seams open.

3. Cut vest pattern pieces out of lining fabric.

4. Pin and baste marbled strips to lining pieces, wrong sides together. Butt strips together until pattern pieces are completely covered, using leftover scraps to fill in small areas.

5. Trim excess marbled fabric around outer edges of lining pieces.

6. Cover butted edges of fabric with bias strips, topstitching close to edges.

7. Complete construction of vest, according to pattern directions. Bind all raw edges with bias binding.

Tips from the designer

■ An alternative method is to attach the marbled silk pieces to a lightweight foundation fabric that will be hidden by the vest lining. Stitch the silk to the foundation fabric strip by strip, right sides together, and press the seams flat before moving on to the next strip. By attaching the marbled strips to a hidden foundation fabric, you can construct a traditional lined vest, instead of using braid or binding to finish raw edges. If your marbled silk is very lightweight or sheer, this method also provides a little more body to the finished garment.

■ When you're experimenting with a new technique in a class, take risks and try anything! For this vest shown here, I marbled a checked silk fabric instead of the usual solid. The underlying grid in the fabric adds a really nice quality to the marbled sections, as if you are peering through a window screen at a magical landscape.

Plan for the Week

Monday

~~~

Tuesday

~~~

Wednesday
Pretreat fabrics as needed.

Thursday
Cut out vest lining or foundation fabric, according to pattern layout.

Friday
Cut marbled fabrics into pieces and reassemble in interesting arrangements.

Saturday
Attach marbled strips to lining or foundation fabric; begin vest construction.

Sunday
Complete vest construction.

For quick and easy construction, butt the strips of marbled fabric together and cover the raw edges with contrasting bias binding. The original checked design of the fabric provides an interesting underlying grid after it is marbled.

Coat Of Many Choices
D E S I G N E R
Piper Hubbell Robinson

Add or subtract a coordinating piece to this easy coat for versatile all-season go-anywhere flair.

Materials and supplies

- Pattern for simple unlined coat

- Thick-pile fleece, in amount required by pattern

- Thin fleece, in amounts required by vest patterns (see below)

- Medium-stretch single knit, 1½-2 yards (1.4-1.85 m)

- Separating zipper for front of coat

- Sewing thread in color suitable for zigzag topstitching

Design details

The designer recommends choosing a coat pattern that provides plenty of room underneath for your regular clothing, the vests you will be making, or other additional layers. The ensemble shown here is based on a man's coat pattern that was altered to meet a smaller woman's needs.

■ Re-sizing a man's pattern is not difficult; you may simply need to down-size some measurements. First, check the shoulder by measuring the shoulder length of a favorite well-fitting coat, from neckline to armhole, and make adjustments as needed.

■ You may need to shorten the sleeves; measure the sleeve length of a favorite coat or jacket and add 2" (5 cm) for the cuff. Depending on your preferences, you may also want to lengthen or shorten the overall body of the coat.

■ Consider adding 2-3" (5-7.5 cm) in width at the bottom side seams of the coat front and back, tapering to the original seamline 2" (5 cm) below the armhole.

■ Check the hip measurement to make sure it will accommodate your body shape, plus ease.

Construction details

1. The designer first eliminated the original center front extensions of the man's coat pattern and created rectangular pockets to stitch to the coat fronts. To determine pocket placement, measure down from the base of the armhole on a favorite coat or jacket to the top of the pocket; then, measure the width of the opening.

2. Make the vest patterns by tracing the coat pattern pieces, shortening fronts and back to the desired length. To make the vests large enough to be worn over the coat, sew ¼" (6 mm) seams, instead of the standard ⅝" (1.5 cm).

3. Use the single knit to trim and bind the front opening and raw seam edges. Cut strips 2-2½" (5-6.5 cm) wide. Fold strip in half and sew to wrong side of fabric. Trim seam allowance to ¼" (6 mm); fold over seam and topstitch in zigzag on right side, so the seam allowance is sandwiched inside the folded strip. NOTE: Apply the knit trim to the center front opening before attaching the separating zipper.

4. Trim vests in the same manner, leaving side seam and center back slits for ease of movement. Finish edges with a machine blanket stitch, and add front ties to the short vest.

5. For an easy scarf to complete the ensemble, cut a simple fleece rectangle and slash the ends to form fringe.

Tips from the designer

■ Before applying the single knit trim, practice various zigzag widths and lengths on scrap fabric, to determine the best settings on your machine.

Plan for the Week

Monday

Pretreat fabrics.

Tuesday

Lay out, cut, and mark coat pattern.

Wednesday

Make two new vest patterns based on coat pattern.

Thursday

Lay out, cut, and mark vest patterns.

Friday

Begin coat and vest construction.

Saturday

Continue coat and vest construction.

Sunday

Complete coat and vests; make fringed scarf.

Artistic Inspiration
DESIGNER
Fradele Feld

Inspiring paintings and other works of art can be successfully reinterpreted in fabric and appliqué. for your own unique artistic expression.

Materials and supplies

- Favorite vest pattern, preferably one without darts

- Assorted fabrics, to equal yardage required by pattern

- Lining fabric, as required by pattern

- Optional batting, flannel, muslin, or thin fabric for quilted version

- Matching, contrasting, rayon embroidery, or decorative threads

- Tracing supplies

- Tear-away or fusible stabilizer, as desired

- Notions required by pattern

Design and construction details

1. Select your inspiration source from an art book, museum catalog, postcard, calendar, idea book, or your own sketches.

2. Cut out a simple vest front and back in miniature from heavy paper or card stock. Position this template with vest-shaped cut-outs on top of your inspiration source and move it around until you see a pleasing arrangement of shapes and colors appear in the cut-out areas. This is the design you will want to re-create on your life-size vest.

3. Re-draw and/or enlarge the original design to fit your vest pattern pieces.

4. Make copies of the enlarged design shapes and cut them out; move them around on the vest pattern pieces to see if the vest pattern needs any adjustment to accommodate the design. For example, you may want to change the shape of the neckline or hemline, or lengthen the vest so the overall design will complement the shape of the vest.

5. Use the cut-out design shapes as pattern pieces, and cut them out of assorted fabrics according to the original inspiration source; if desired, stabilize fabrics before cutting out shapes. Try to approximate the colors of the original design in your choice and placement of fabrics (see Designer Tip below).

6. Pin-baste, thread-baste, or fuse design shapes to vest pieces and stitch in place according to the original design. You can satin stitch around the raw edges of each shape, using matching, contrasting, or decorative threads. Or, fold the raw edges under and hand-stitch or edgestitch in place. If you fold the raw edges under, don't forget to add a small seam allowance to all shapes.

7. If you are not quilting the appliquéd vest pieces, proceed with vest and lining construction.

8. If you choose to quilt the vest pieces, do it before putting the vest together. When all design shapes are attached to the vest pieces, complete the quilting by hand or machine, with contrasting or decorative threads as desired. Compare quilted pieces to original vest pattern pieces and trim excess fabric around edges of pattern pieces. Proceed with vest construction.

Tips from the designer

■ Part of the reason why a particular painting or art work inspires you is because of the artist's arrangement of colors. Therefore, when selecting fabrics for your wearable interpretation, try to choose similar colors or go for prints that give the feeling of the artist's colors.

■ Even though you're working in fabric, you are composing the finished piece just as an artist composes with paint, layer by layer,. Therefore, watch out for darker colors that may show through lighter colors placed on top. You might have to trim away some of the dark-colored fabric underneath.

■ If you want the vest to have a quilted look, cut the vest fronts and back a little larger than the pattern pieces. The quilting will draw the fabric in a bit, and you can trim away any excess before constructing the vest. Also, if you use a thin batting or lightweight interlining, you will get a nice dimensional quality to the vest.

FOR A WONDERFUL, YET HIDDEN, TOUCH OF CONVENIENCE, MAKE A LITTLE HANDKERCHIEF POCKET IN THE VEST LINING.

Plan for the Week

Monday

Tuesday
Pretreat fabrics.

Wednesday
Make miniature vest template and move around on top of inspiration source, to determine design; enlarge design.

Thursday
Lay out, cut, and mark vest; interface appropriate pieces; cut out enlarged design shapes and arrange on vest pieces.

Friday
Cut design shapes out of assorted fabrics; appliqué to vest pieces.

Saturday
Quilt appliquéd vest pieces, if desired; begin vest and lining construction.

Sunday
Complete vest construction.

Cow Town High Style
DESIGNER
M. Luanne Carson

Put some fun back in your sewing life with this happy vest that's a snap to make out of synthetic fleece or faux fur.

Design and construction details

The designer wanted to create a garment that would bring a smile to her face, and to everyone who sees her wearing it.

■ Synthetic fleece is easy to work with, and very "forgiving." On this vest, the designer simply turned under the raw edges and topstitched them in place with a narrow zigzag. An alternative method is to serge the raw edges with Woolly Nylon in both the upper and lower loopers, for a bound edge.

■ By using a wide fabric, she was able to cut the vest front and back in one piece, eliminating side seams. It was quick work to stitch just the two shoulder seams.

■ She attached the two-part buckle fastener to the vest fronts with synthetic suede.

Windows On A Colorful World

DESIGNER
Barbara Fugazzotto

Create the colorful jeweled effect of stained-glass windows with this easy fabric piecing technique.

Materials and supplies

- Favorite vest pattern, preferably one without darts
- Pre-washed muslin, to equal yardage required by pattern
- Assorted related fabrics, to equal yardage required by pattern
- Lining fabric, as required by pattern
- Assorted fabric scraps for window facings and backgrounds
- Decorative button
- Construction-weight paper
- Rotary cutter and mat, or cutting supplies
- Notions required by pattern

Construction details

1. Cut pattern pieces out of muslin. They will be the foundation pieces for the strip piecing.

2. Cut strips of desired widths from assorted related fabrics.

3. Arrange strips on a flat surface, to get an arrangement of color, pattern, and width that you like.

4. Starting at one side of strip arrangement, stitch a band to corresponding edge of foundation piece. Lay strip open and press seam flat.

5. Right sides together, stitch next strip to the first; lay second strip open and press.

6. Continue, strip by strip, until all muslin foundation pieces have been covered.

7. Steam press vest pieces and stay stitch around all outer edges, through all thicknesses.

8. Cut assorted window shapes from heavy or construction-weight paper.

9. Cut window shapes out of facing fabric, allowing at least 1" (2.5 cm) extra around all edges.

10. Determine placement of window shapes on vest pieces. Pin the facing fabric pieces to right side of vest pieces, according to window placement.

11. Place paper window shapes on top of facing fabrics, and trace around paper patterns.

12. Stitch along traced lines, beginning and ending along a side, so corners are securely stitched.

13. Cut out window, leaving 1/4" (6 mm) seam allowances. Clip into corners and curves.

14. Turn facing fabric to inside, through the window, and press. Consider letting the facing fabric show a bit, like a frame around the window.

15. Place a scrap of background fabric, or a collage of various background fabrics behind each window. Pin in place.

16. Topstitch around window opening.

17. Assemble and line vest according to pattern instructions.

Tips from the designer

- This vest is a great way to use treasured scraps of beautiful fabrics, both for the custom strip-pieced yardage and the colorful fabric "jewels" behind the window openings. You can even use bits of lace and trim inside the windows, or decorate them from the outside with buttons or sequins.

■ For a nice finishing touch, make a window inside the vest at the back neckline, and top it off with your own designer label.

FUGAZZOTTO

Plan for the Week

Monday

∾∾∾

Tuesday

∾∾∾

Wednesday
Pretreat fabrics.

Thursday
Cut out vest pattern from muslin; cut and arrange strips for piecing.

Friday
Strip-piece yardage for vest and stitch to muslin foundation.

Saturday
Make window patterns; face and cut out windows; attach window backgrounds; begin vest construction.

Sunday
Complete vest construction; make buttonhole and sew on button; embellish windows as desired.

All-Weather Microfiber
DESIGNER
Mary S. Parker

A microfiber raincoat is handy in spring and summer, but add an insulated zip-out lining and you've got a year-round fashion.

Design details

The designer started with a pattern for an unlined coat with two-part raglan sleeve; the front facing extended only part of the way around the neckline to the sleeve shoulder seam, and there was no back facing.

■ She selected a versatile microfiber fabric for the unlined coat, for easy care and comfort in wet weather. For cold-season practicality, she designed and made a zip-out insulated lining.

■ For the machine-washable lining, she layered a light-weight Thinsulate insulation and silk-like polyester print. A separating zipper guarantees easy removal.

■ To ensure that the coat would not separate in front when walking, the designer added walking ease to the front pattern piece before cutting out the fronts. By the method she used (see illustration), she achieved about 2½-3" (6.5-7.5 cm) ease at the hemline of the coat.

Construction details

To add walking ease:

1. Tape tracing paper or blank pattern tissue to the center front edge of the coat front pattern piece.

2. Position one end of a yardstick on the center front, ⅝" (1.5 cm) below the neck edge. Rotate the opposite end of the yardstick out until it is 1½" (4 cm) away from center front.

3. Trace a line along the yardstick. Slide yardstick along the traced line to the bottom of the pattern piece, and extend the traced line to the bottom edge. Connect the bottom point of the traced line with the bottom edge of the pattern piece, matching any curve of the pattern. An alternative method is to slash the front pattern piece, from hem to neck edge, and spread apart the desired amount. See illustration.

4. Use the new traced line as the center front cutting line. Even though this new line is slightly off-grain, you will not be able to tell when the coat is made. The additional width along the front edge provides enough fabric ease that the coat fronts will not separate when you walk or move.

To adjust the coat pattern for an added lining:

1. Lay the coat front and sleeve front pattern pieces on a flat surface and pin them together along the sleeve seam-line from the neck edge outward for about 5" (12.5 cm).

2. Lay the front facing pattern piece on top, matching center fronts and neck edges of the facing and coat front patterns. Trace along the outer edge of the facing pattern onto the coat front pattern.

3. Rotate the front facing pattern so that it now matches the neck edge of the sleeve front. Trace along the outer edge of the facing pattern onto the sleeve front pattern. This will be the cutting line for the lining pieces.

4. Remove the front facing pattern and set aside; un-pin front and sleeve pieces.

5. For a back neck facing, lay coat back and sleeve back pattern pieces on a flat surface and pin them together along the sleeve seamline from the neck edge outward for about 5" (12.5 cm).

6. Place some tracing paper or blank pattern tissue over the pinned-together coat and sleeve backs. Trace the back neck edge curve and the sleeve center seamline.

7. Draw a curved lower edge the same width from the neck edge as the front facing was at the shoulder line. Cut out this new back facing pattern.

8. Lay back facing pattern on top of pinned-together coat and sleeve backs, and trace along the outer edge as you did on the fronts.

To make patterns for lining pieces:

1. Lay tracing paper or blank pattern tissue on top of front, back, sleeve front, and sleeve back pattern pieces.

2. Trace along all outside edges and the new cutting lines you drew above.

Notes about coat construction:

1. Because you will be attaching the coat's front facing pieces to the new lining, remember to add seam allowances to the outer edges of the front facing pattern when you cut the fashion fabric.

2. Cut out both layers of the insulated lining separately, and then baste all matching pieces together around outside edges. Handle as one during construction.

3. When cutting out the lining pieces for the coat back, ignore the extension for the kick pleat. Instead, place the seamline of the coat back along the fold of the lining fabrics when cutting. Then, slash the lining along the fold the same distance as the kick pleat. Finish or bind raw edges of the slash.

4. To keep the polyester lining fabric from sliding and hanging below the insulation at the hem edge, channel quilt the two layers together by stitching three parallel rows across the

MAKE A ZIP-OUT INSULATED LINING FOR ANY COAT PATTERN THAT HAS A FRONT FACING AND YOU GET A FOUR-SEASON FASHION. USE WASHABLE FABRICS FOR THE LINING LAYERS TO CUT DOWN ON DRY-CLEANING BILLS.

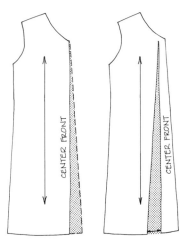

Adding walking ease to a front-opening garment will keep it from spreading apart while you walk or move. Add it at the center front hemline, tapering to zero at the neck seamline (left), or slash and spread the pattern piece at the hemline, tapering to zero at the neckline (right) or any point that keeps the pattern piece flat.

fronts and backs, 2" (5 cm), 4" (10 cm), and 6" (15 cm) from the bottom edge.

5. Before inserting the zipper, stitch around the outer edge of the assembled front and back lining, ¾" (2 cm) from the edge. Trim to ⅛" (3 mm). Stitch double-fold bias tape on top of previous stitching, stitch opposite fold of the bias tape to the zipper tape, and then attach lining/zipper to coat's front and back facing. The use of bias tape eliminates the extra bulk of a seam allowance along

AFTER THE COAT AND BELT WERE COMPLETED, THE DESIGNER DECIDED THAT THE INSULATED LINING MADE THE FINAL FASHION TOO BULKY WHEN CINCHED IN AROUND THE WAIST. INSTEAD OF DISCARDING THE BELT AND CUTTING OFF THE BELT CARRIERS, SHE DECIDED TO USE THE BELT AS A PURELY DECORATIVE TOUCH AND BUTTON IT TO THE BACK OVERLAY.

the zipper, which can be quite hefty if you use a thick insulating layer.

Tips from the designer

■ Buy the longest separating zipper you can find. I would have liked one longer than the 60" (162 cm) zipper in this coat, so it could have reached all the way around from left front hem to right front hem. As it is, it extends only to about knee-length.

■ When calculating how much fabric to buy for the lining and insulation, it's best to make your lining pattern pieces first and then measure how much you'll need. However, a good rule of thumb is to buy ¾-1 yard (.7-.95 m) less than the fashion fabric.

■ Microfiber has a tendency to pucker, especially when sewing long seams. To help reduce puckering, cut the fabric slightly offgrain (10 percent or so), and use Micro-Tex needles, which are especially made for sewing on these types of fabrics.

Plan for the Week

Monday

∿∿∿

Tuesday
Pretreat fabrics.

Wednesday
Trace and make back facing and lining pattern pieces.

Thursday
Lay out, cut, and mark coat; interface appropriate pieces; begin coat construction.

Friday
Continue coat construction; cut out lining pieces and baste together.

Saturday
Complete coat construction; assemble lining.

Sunday
Insert lining and zipper; hem coat; make buttonholes and sew on buttons.

Vintage Fashion DESIGNER
Karen Swing

Give an antique tablecloth a new lease on life by re-styling it as an up-to-date fashion.

Design and construction details

The designer started with a 60" x 60" (152 x 152 cm) white linen tablecloth with a decorative jacquard border, and refashioned it into a go-with-everything jacket.

■ Because the well-worn linen tablecloth would not stay squared during cutting and sewing, she starched it heavily before laying it out to cut. The starch gave the fabric enough body to keep the grainlines squared, and it washed right out after the jacket was completed.

■ During pattern layout, she positioned the front opening of the jacket along the tablecloth's decorative border to take advantage of the fabric's beautiful woven design.

■ She used white cotton thread for garment construction and dyed the completed jacket, to cover a discolored area of the tablecloth. When dyed, the thread matches perfectly!

Tips from the designer

■ Old or damaged tablecloths and bedspreads that you find at the flea market or in the family trunk are perfect candidates for recycling. Try to balance the size of the pattern or decorative border with the garment pieces, and look carefully for damaged or faded areas before cutting.

■ Starching a washable fabric before cutting and sewing makes it so much easier to work with. This also works well with slippery silks and rayons, but be sure they are washable.

■ When dyeing a completed garment, use cold water dyes. Cotton thread is rarely preshrunk, so hot water would cause the seams to draw up.

Ethnic Embellishment
DESIGNER
Joneen M. Sargent

Beautiful pieces of ethnic textiles can be artfully appliquéd to a basic jacket for an international look.

Materials and supplies

- Simple box jacket pattern

- Fashion fabric and lining, as required by pattern

- Assorted appliqués, embroideries, or ethnic textiles

- Rayon machine embroidery thread

- Fusible web product

- Heat-removable stabilizer

- Assorted machine embroidery needles and sewing machine feet

- Assorted decorative yarns for couching

- Notions required by pattern

Tips from the designer

- Ethnic textiles, even small ones, can be incorporated into your own original fashions in wonderful ways. I love these Hmong appliqué squares, but their regimented look and precise detail made me yearn for some random playfulness. The couched yarns in a random pattern filled the bill for me.

- Take the time to experiment with your machine's stitch capabilities and a variety of threads on swatches that have the same number of fabric layers as the actual jacket. Some of the techniques I used in this jacket are sewing with two different threads in one needle, twin needle stitching with different color threads in each needle, varying stitch width and length, and couching yarns with a zigzag stitch.

Construction details

1. Trace jacket pattern pieces onto fashion fabric. Roughly cut pieces out, about 1" (2.5 cm) larger all around than each traced pattern piece. The excess fabric allows for some drawing-in caused by the decorative stitching. The manipulation of the fabric also requires the bulk of the uncut pieces.

2. Position appliqués or embroideries on jacket fabric in a pleasing arrangement; fold raw edges under and apply to fabric with fusible web.

3. Position stabilizer on wrong side of fabric beneath appliqués; machine embroider around edges of appliqués, using rayon thread and a variety of stitch techniques (see Designer Tip below).

4. Remove stabilizer according to package directions.

5. Trim fabric rectangles along traced pattern lines and assemble jacket according to instructions.

"Several years ago, I attended a craft show and fell in love with these hand-stitched fabric appliqués made by a Hmong woman from Thailand. I snatched up as many as I could afford and admired them until I figured out how to use them in one of my garments. In honor and respect for the woman who made them, I left her works of art untouched."

Plan for the Week

Monday

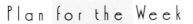

Tuesday
Pretreat jacket fabric.

Wednesday
Make trial swatches to test stitch options and different thread-needle combinations.

Thursday
Trace pattern pieces onto fabric; roughly cut out.

Friday
Apply couched threads and textiles to jacket pieces; begin decorative stitching.

Saturday
Complete decorative stitching; trim pieces to fit pattern; begin jacket construction.

Sunday
Complete jacket construction.

Pieced Rhapsody in Blue
DESIGNER
Margaret Richardson

Gather your favorite fabric scraps and small pieces for this colorful mosaic of paper pieced blocks that are tied together with a denim blue cotton.

Materials and supplies

■ Vest pattern of choice, preferably one without darts

■ Assorted fashion fabrics, preferably of similar weight and body, for paper piecing (select fabrics to achieve a balance of colors, textures, and patterns)

■ Coordinating fabric of choice (the designer used denim-colored cotton)

■ Lining fabric, as required by pattern

■ Coordinating or contrasting bias tape

■ Rotary cutter, mat, and ruler, or cutting supplies of choice

■ Roll of narrow fusible web (optional)

■ Decorative buttons

■ Notions required by pattern

■ Graph paper

Construction details

1. Draw desired patchwork designs on graph paper or select paper piecing patterns at your local quilt shop. Make enough copies of each patchwork design for each design repeat on the vest. The designer used the flying geese, square in a square, and fan patterns.

2. Each patchwork design is created in a numerical sequence, so number the patch components in order. See Figure 1.

3. Center the fabric piece for patch #1, wrong side of fabric to back side of paper pattern. Pin in place on the top side of paper pattern (side with lines drawn on it), making sure the fabric extends at least ¼" (6 mm) beyond all edges of patch #1.

4. Turn paper pattern over again and place the fabric piece for patch #2 right side down on the fabric for patch #1. Hold fabrics in place and turn the paper pattern over.

5. Machine sew along the line between patches #1 and #2, starting and stopping one stitch beyond the ends of the drawn line. You may trim seam allowances within the patch to ¼" (6 mm), but do not trim any seam allowances along the outside edges of the entire block until later.

6. Place the block on ironing board, fabric side up. Flip the patch #2 fabric open and press seam flat.

7. Sew patch #3 to patch #2 in the same manner, and proceed for all other patches, until the block is complete.

8. Repeat with additional copies of the paper pattern until you have enough blocks for strip or section.

9. Leave the paper patterns on until you have sewn the blocks together and trimmed the edges to ¼" (6 mm). When completed, remove paper and press. The patchwork strips are now ready to be incorporated into your vest.

10. Cut vest pattern pieces from coordinating fashion fabric. Position patchwork strips on vest fronts and back, as desired. Baste in place with thread or fusible web. Cover raw edges of patchwork strips with bias tape and topstitch in place.

11. Assemble and line vest, according to pattern instructions.

Tips from the designer

■ Paper piecing is a wonderful method of achieving the look of precise patchwork without templates, precision cutting, or perfect ¼" (6 mm) seam allowances. It's a simple sew, flip, and press method. If you can sew on a line, you can do machine paper piecing.

■ When sewing the fabrics to the paper patterns, use a short stitch length. This makes it easier to remove the paper later.

■ Sew the blocks in assembly line fashion, to speed the process up: sew a bunch, flip a bunch, press a bunch.

■ If some of the fabrics you want to use in your piecework mosaic don't have much body to them, lightly interface or starch them so they will be easier to work with.

■ Look for interesting objects for use as decorative buttons, including shells, coins, stones, beads, and bits of jewelry. Simply glue the object to an inexpensive flat button with a shank. I glued these pretty ceramic disks to the ends of a short loop of leather boot lacing, and stitched the loop to the opposite vest front. The disks slip easily through inseam buttonholes created right down the center front.

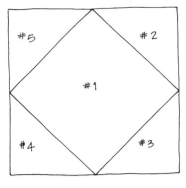

FIG. 1 SEQUENCE FOR PIECING "SQUARE IN SQUARE" PATTERN.

Plan for the Week

Monday
Pretreat fabrics; make copies of paper patterns; organize fabrics.

Tuesday
Begin paper piecing.

Wednesday
Continue paper piecing.

Thursday
Continue paper piecing.

Friday
Complete pieced blocks and sew together into strips.

Saturday
Cut out vest pattern; attach pieced strips to vest fronts and back; begin vest construction.

Sunday
Complete vest construction; make buttonholes and attach buttons.

Pick-A-Pocket

DESIGNER
Beth Karjala

Everyday items, such as these interesting dish towels, can be cut apart and reassembled into exciting wearable designs.

Materials and supplies

- Assorted coordinating cotton dish towels or cotton fabric, to equal 4 yards (3.7 m)

- Cutting supplies, or rotary cutter and mat

- Matching or contrasting thread

Design and construction details

The designer cut four 1-yard (.95-m) striped cotton dish towels into squares, and then in half to form triangles. She arranged the striped triangles into a design and serged them together. She then serged smaller triangles together to form squares and stitched them on top in a diamond arrangement, leaving one side of each open for a pocket.

1. To size the garment, take hip measurements and add 6" (15 cm) for garment width. Determine desired length.

2. Cut 9" (23 cm) squares out of assorted fabrics, enough to equal measurements taken above.

3. Cut squares in half diagonally to form triangles.

4. Arrange the pieces into a pleasing design for the coat back and front.

5. Serge the pieces together, shaping the neckline as desired, and leaving the armholes and front open.

6. To add structural support and make the garment reversible, cut and serge the edges of several 3" (7.5 cm), 4" (10 cm), and 5" (12.5 cm) squares; machine-stitch them on the inside wherever the garment's serged corners meet.

7. For the pockets, cut several squares; cut them diagonally into triangles, mix them up, and reassemble them into squares. Serge around outside edges.

8. Position them in a diamond arrangement on coat fronts and pin in place (see illustration).

9. Machine stitch diamonds to fronts, leaving one side unstitched to form pocket opening.

Tips from the designer

- Serging the edges of pieces cut on the bias creates a ripple effect, which can contrast nicely with the monotony of so many straight edges.

- The serged thread tails add an interesting surface texture, so I let them hang loose.

Plan for the Week

Monday
~~~~~
### Tuesday
~~~~~
Wednesday
Pretreat fabrics; determine measurements.
Thursday
Cut squares and triangles; reassemble squares from assorted triangles.
Friday
Assemble garment fronts and back from serged squares.
Saturday
Make small squares and stitch to inside of garment, over intersections of serged squares.
Sunday
Make pocket squares and stitch to fronts.

FOUR DIFFERENT STRIPED FABRICS, LIKE THESE COTTON DISH TOWELS, CAN BE CUT APART AND REASSEMBLED TO PRODUCE A TRULY UNIQUE LOOK. FREE-HANGING THREAD TAILS ADD SURFACE TEXTURE.

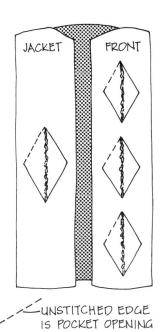

JACKET FRONT

UNSTITCHED EDGE IS POCKET OPENING

"Creatively placed pockets can become the most intriguing part of a garment's design."

Tulip Swizzle

DESIGNER

Judith S. Plucker

Here's a quick and easy jacket design that adds a touch of colorful flash to any ensemble.

Materials and supplies

- Pattern for simple, untailored jacket
- Fashion fabric of choice, as required by pattern
- 1 yard (.95 m) contrasting fabric of choice, for floral appliqués and bias strips
- Lightweight fusible stabilizer
- Thread to match both fabrics
- Tracing paper
- Notions required by pattern

Construction details

1. Draw a simple design of stylized flowers on tracing paper and adjust it until you are satisfied with the look.

2. Cut out jacket pieces and sew together at the shoulder seams. Attach sleeves to jacket at shoulders, but leave underarm seams unstitched until later.

3. Cut 2½" (6.5 cm) bias strips of contrasting fabric. Piece strips together end to end, to make a strip long enough to go around front and neckline opening from hem to hem. Make a second strip long enough for jacket's bottom edge and two shorter strips for the sleeve hems.

4. Fuse stabilizer to wrong side of contrasting fabric; transfer drawings to stabilizer. Cut out the flower shapes, position on jacket fronts and back as desired, and satin stitch around all edges. Satin stitch the stems between flowers.

5. Stitch jacket side and underarm seams and attach bias bindings to raw edges.

Tips from the designer

- Here's a handy way to position the cut-out appliqués on the jacket exactly as they were on your drawing. With a straight pin, punch holes in your tracing paper design along the lines you drew. Pin or tape the punched paper to the jacket and dust it with white chalk; the chalk will settle through the holes and form a clear, but temporary, guideline for placing the appliqués. Any excess chalk can be easily brushed off.

- You may want to stitch the flower stems first, and then cover the ends with the flower cutouts.

Fashionable First Aid
DESIGNER
Pat Scheible

Resuscitate failed sewing projects with a transplant operation that gives them a beautiful new life.

Design and construction details

The designer saved two sewing accidents with some creative transplant surgery. She explains, "If you're like me, you buy fabrics you love, but you don't always love what you make out of them. I had a striped silk-cotton blouse that was the victim of an inappropriate pattern, and a loosely-woven silk tweed that suffered from various stitching mishaps. What to do with two casualties out of fabrics I loved? Save both patients and make a vest!"

■ She salvaged as much vital fabric as possible from the two failed projects. She used the striped silk for bias binding, vest back, design accents, and front ties. She used the mis-stitched silk tweed for the vest fronts and back lining.

■ She then used the striped silk bias binding to finish the vest's raw edges. For a smooth result, she gently curved the bias binding and steamed it into shape before topstitching in place.

Tips from the designer

■ Even after years of sewing, when we're older and wiser, accidents can still happen. Don't give these mistakes up for dead. With a little ingenuity, you can bring them back to life.

■ Invest in a bias tape maker. These nifty notions come in assorted sizes and make it so easy to produce your own bias edgings, bindings, and button loops.

THE DESIGNER RECYCLED THESE TWO BEAUTIFUL FABRICS FROM ONE COMPLETED GARMENT SHE DIDN'T LIKE AND ANOTHER ONE THAT HAD STITCHING PROBLEMS. WITH SOME CREATIVE THINKING, UNSUCCESSFUL PROJECTS CAN FIND NEW LIFE.

Checkerboard Puzzle

DESIGNER
M. Luanne Carson

For truly unique style, the designer composed this jacket as a painter would a canvas, in a fascinating puzzle of visual surprises.

■ The two plaids appeared too inconsistent in size when placed next to each other, so she serged a tuck through the red blocks of the larger plaid on the coat front and topstitched a narrow bias band of the small plaid through the red blocks on the coat back.

■ The designer added new shapes to connect and relate to the shapes already attached to the jacket. For example, the back design was visually connected to the front by a swoop of the black corduroy around the right front at the hipline.

■ Several design features were added for pure decoration, such as an occasional black button and a shiny black triangular tab at the upper left shoulder. The finished garment would look "empty" without them.

Tips from the designer

■ Experiment with design characteristics inherent in the fabric for creative possibilities. In this jacket, the ribs of the corduroy and the plaid design of the flannel provided many interesting linear elements to play with. Mixing the horizontal, vertical, and diagonal directions of the fabrics gave me numerous options for visual effect.

■ This spontaneous type of sewing is so much like painting. You evaluate the "canvas" or garment-in-progress and add elements that relate to what's already there.

■ The best part about this artful jacket is that it's also washable, lightweight, and a joy to wear. By choosing easy-care, comfortable fabrics, the result is a wonderful combination of creativity and function.

Design and construction details

The designer started with an innovative coat design that had broad expanses of fabric uncluttered by darts, pleats, or other construction details. This allowed her to creatively piece four fabrics (two solid corduroys and two plaid flannels) and sculpt a distinctive garment layer by layer.

Ribbon Hearts
DESIGNER
Karen M. Bennett

Make pretty tatted baskets of silk ribbon flowers to decorate a luscious velvet vest. This is one original fashion you'll never find in ready-to-wear.

Design and construction details

The designer enjoys tatting, silk ribbon embroidery, and sewing. She combines all three techniques to individualize this basic vest pattern.

■ She tatted a large and small basket, and attached each one to a vest front with invisible nylon sewing thread. She then embellished each basket with silk ribbon embroidery, using a variety of colors and stitches, including French knots, whipped roses, and seed stitches.

■ For accents, she used glass beads and a ribbon bow secured in place with beads.

Tips from the designer

■ When sewing with velvet, remember that the fabric has a nap. Cut all pattern pieces in the same direction, or different pieces will appear to be slightly different colors. Stabilize buttonholes in velvet with adding machine tape or notebook paper before sewing them. And always use a velvet pressing board or thick terrycloth towel when pressing napped fabric.

■ It's an absolute must that you press the silk ribbon before using it.

■ Glass beads make wonderful accents, because they reflect the light.

For more information about tatting and silk ribbon embroidery:

Jones, Rebecca. *The Complete Book of Tatting*. London: Dryad Press Limited, 1985.

Montano, Judith Baker. *The Art of Silk Ribbon Embroidery*. Lafayette, California: C&T Publishing, 1993.

Vested In Gold

DESIGNER
Thelma P. Matthews

The warm and lovely glow of gold emanates from this extra special vest with laced sides.

Design and construction details

Inspiration comes from everywhere! This fashion was inspired by the orange utility vests that construction workers wear.

■ To complement the gold-painted fashion fabric, the designer cut a collar from metallic organdy. She added support to the sheer fabric with a washable stabilizer and then couched gold and black decorative cords on top.

■ She lined the vest with the same stabilized organdy as the collar, for consistency from inside to outside.

■ For a different touch, she eliminated the typical stitched side seams. Instead, she connected vest fronts and back with the gold and black braid laced through golden grommets. The final touch is a glittering frog closure of gold braid.

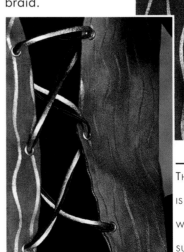

THE GLOWING, TRANSLUCENT COLLAR IS CUT FROM METALLIC ORGANDY WITH WASHABLE STABILIZER ADDED TO SUPPORT THE COUCHED DECORATIVE CORDS. YOU CAN SEE JUST A HINT OF THE VEST FABRIC THROUGH THE COLLAR, GIVING A NICE DIMENSIONAL QUALITY TO THE OVERALL GARMENT.

Variations On A Theme
DESIGNER
Barbara Fugazzotto

Create two distinct fashions with a few changes to a simple pattern, some decorative appliqués, and the interplay between two sides of the same fabric.

Design and construction details

The designer used an ethnic kimono pattern as a starting point for a dramatic experiment in color mixing and appliqué design in two jacket lengths.

■ She made two adjustments to the kimono pattern, according to her style and fitting preferences. First, for a more flattering shoulder line than the kimono's boxy look, she redrew the shoulder line to slope from the original neckline down to a point 2" (5 cm) below the pattern's shoulder point. Then, she re-curved and tapered the underarm sleeve seam to take out some of the bulk of the kimono sleeve (see illustration).

■ Because the fabric is two-sided, she experimented with the right side/wrong side and light/dark possibilities in the appliqué design of both the short jacket and long coat. She drew various arrangements of shapes and, when satisfied with one, made two copies of it: one copy to cut up as pattern pieces for the individual shapes and the other copy to remind herself of how the composition goes together.

■ All appliqué shapes were "cut out" of the fabric with a serger rather than scissors, to save time and increase efficiency; once cut out, the raw edges of the shapes are already finished. The designer used various combinations of colored threads in the loopers and needles of the serger to both enhance and coordinate with the fashion fabric. She calls this method "color serging."

■ The color-serged appliqué shapes were arranged on the jacket/coat fronts and backs according to the photocopy of the entire design composition. Slight modifications were made, all shapes pinned in place, and then she zigzagged around the edges in yet another coordinating thread color.

THE DESIGNER USED THE RIGHT AND WRONG SIDES OF THE FABRIC, FRINGED SELVAGE, AND ASSORTED COLOR COMBINATIONS OF LOOPER AND NEEDLE THREADS TO CREATE INTERESTING DECORATIVE EFFECTS.

APPLIQUÉ SHAPES DON'T HAVE TO BE COMPLETELY STITCHED TO THE BACK-
GROUND. FOR EXAMPLE, THIS DECORATIVE FLAP OF SHAPED FABRIC ADDS A
NICE THREE-DIMENSIONAL QUALITY TO THE BACK YOKE.

■ Finally, she sewed meandering lines of colored stitching throughout the design, using zigzag and straight stitching, and steam pressed all shapes before assembling the jacket and coat.

■ As a final touch, she stitched an appliqué shape to the inside of the back neckband and topped it off with her own designer label.

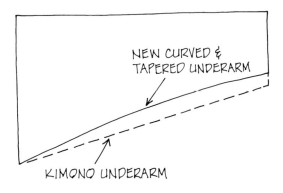

NEW CURVED &
TAPERED UNDERARM

KIMONO UNDERARM

RE-SHAPING KIMONO SLEEVE

THE DESIGNER PREFERS A MORE SHAPED AND TAPERED SLEEVE THAN THE
TRADITIONAL KIMONO STYLE, SO SHE GENTLY RE-CURVED THE UNDERARM
SEAM TO PROVIDE THE DESIRED LOOK AND FIT.

Tips from the designer

■ Study the pattern of your fabric for design motifs to use in your appliqué compositions. Note the shapes already there and use them in your overall plan. If the fabric pattern is largely geometric, your design composition will be different than if the shapes are more organic.

■ Experiment with thread color combinations, and mix and match them in the loopers and needles, or needle and bobbin, of your machines. Let your fabric suggest colors, but don't be afraid to get wild. Sometimes the color you think will definitely not work will be just the right one.

■ To hide thread ends, leave long tails and use a large-eye needle to pass them under the fabric's weave for 1" (2.5 cm) or so.

■ If the selvage is nicely patterned or fringed, think about how you can incorporate it into the design. Selvages can add some visual interest, and they're already bound and finished!

Plan for the Week

Monday

∾∾∾∾

Tuesday

Pretreat fabric samples; experiment with thread colors and stitch combinations.

Wednesday

Pretreat fabric; begin appliqué design.

Thursday

Finalize appliqué design; make two photocopies; cut one photocopy apart to make pattern pieces for appliqué shapes.

Friday

Cut out appliqué shapes and color-serge edges; arrange on garment pieces and pin in place.

Saturday

Stitch appliqué shapes to garment pieces; sew meandering design lines of stitching, as desired; begin garment construction.

Sunday

Complete garment construction.

UPHOLSTERY FABRIC:
A Treasure Trove of Color and Pattern

The designer likes to use upholstery fabrics for unique garments because they are usually very beautiful, rich in color and pattern. They are typically very interesting on both the right and wrong sides, too. However, these hearty fabrics can be stiff and uncomfortable to wear. When looking at these wonderful materials, consider the following:

■ Is it supple enough to conform to the body? Wrap it around your arm like a sleeve, then bend the arm to feel and see how the fabric moves.

■ Is it lightweight enough to be worn comfortably? Feel the weight of a 3-yard (2.75-m) piece. This is what you will carry around when it's a coat or jacket.

■ Is it soft enough to wear against the skin? Wrap it around your neck and feel the texture against your skin.

■ Does the fabric have an interesting wrong side? Will the interaction of wrong side and right side yield unusual design possibilities?

■ Does it have an interesting selvage that could be used as a decorative accent? Fringes and colorful woven edges offer many possibilities.

■ Is there a rubberized or latex-coated surface? If so, don't buy it!

Once you have selected the perfect upholstery fabric for a special garment, cut a 12" (30.5 cm) square, serge the raw edges, and wash the fabric. This removes the sizing, softens the fabric, and alerts you to possible care problems. For example, rayon or silk upholstery won't survive the wash very well; you will have to dry clean the finished garment.

Dry the sample in the dryer until just damp; remove and steam press. Compare the sample to the original yardage. The washing and drying may have created some interesting effects, such as rendering it extra supple or puckering the design. It's nice to know this in advance, so you can work it into your design, if desired.

If the washed samples are acceptable, serge the raw edges of the remaining yardage and pretreat the same way. Then proceed with the design and construction of your unique garment.

Tri-Collar Vest

DESIGNER

Charlotte Redemann

Get plenty of design mileage out of a classic black wool crepe vest with these three snazzy detachable collars.

Materials and supplies

■ Completed collarless vest

■ ½-1 yard (.5-.95 m) selected fabric for detachable collar

■ Fabric for facing or bias band, to which collar will be sewn (This needs to be firm enough to securely hold the collar and snaps, long enough to go around the garment neckline, and wide enough to accommodate the snaps or other fasteners you choose.)

■ Size 1 snaps, hook-and-loop tape, or buttons of choice (The number of fasteners will vary according to the vest's neckline size; they should be placed close enough together to keep the collar from pulling away from the vest.)

■ Paper towels or pattern-making paper

Construction details

1. Choose the type of fastener you will use to attach the collar to the vest. There are several options, including snaps, hook-and-loop tape, and buttons. Snaps are lightweight and nearly invisible. Hook-and-loop tape adds bulk, and therefore is best for lightweight collars. Buttons can be a decorative design feature when visible against the collar fabric; however, they require buttonholes in the facing of each collar.

2. Choose the placement of the selected fasteners on the vest. They can be sewn to the inside (lining) of the vest or the outside fabric. If fasteners are attached to the inside of the vest, an extra layer will be added between the wearer and the garment; additionally, the presence of snaps or buttons inside the vest may be uncomfortable, especially if the vest can also be worn without a detachable collar.

3. To make a basic flat pattern for the detachable collar, pin vest front and back pattern pieces together along the shoulder seams.

4. Lay pattern-making paper or a paper towel on top and, with a soft pencil, trace the vest neckline from the front neckline to center back, and about 3" (7.5 cm) wide, shaping the outer edge parallel to the neckline.

5. Cut out the traced collar pattern and use it as a model for experimenting with different styles. Pin paper

to vest neckline and manipulate to achieve a desirable shape and design. For example, take tiny darts in one area or slash and spread in another, or shape the outer edge in undulating curves or extended points.

6. Using the desired paper pattern, cut and sew the collar, adding seam allowances as needed.

7. Sew the collar to a bias band wide enough to accommodate the selected fasteners or to a shaped facing cut from the flat collar pattern.

8. Attach collar to vest.

For the Snap-On Scarf Collar

1. Pin a length of ⅜" (1 cm) grosgrain ribbon around the vest neckline so that it covers the snaps. Leave any excess ribbon hanging loose at the front opening.

2. Sew snap halves to the ribbon, corresponding to the snap halves on the vest.

3. Put on the vest and arrange a selected scarf around the neckline as desired, pinning it to the vest as you go. Tie a knot or bow in one end of the scarf.

4. Take the vest off. Starting at the front of the vest, hand-tack the scarf to the ribbon lightly but firmly, unpinning as you go. Be sure that the folds and twists are secure, but don't stitch so tightly that the scarf looks nailed down. Snip off any excess ribbon.

5. Sew a snap to the back of the knot or bow, so that the other end of the scarf appears to be tied into the knot.

For the Pintucked Metallic Sheer Collar

1. Cut the basic flat collar pattern about 2" (5 cm) wider than the finished width to allow for trimming the edges later, and about twice as long to accommodate the pintucks. To do this, trace the collar pattern, cut across the pattern in several places, spread the pieces apart, and retrace the pattern.

2. Make narrow tucks across the width of the collar, being careful not to take up too much length in the tucks. Trim the outer edge of the collar into its final shape with pinking shears.

3. Using a large-eye blunt needle, thread strips of assorted fibers and leather through pintucks, leaving a generous tail at each side.

4. Machine stitch along the inner, neckline edge of the collar pattern to secure the colored strands. Trim the neckline edge into its final shape, and bind with the bias strip.

5. Attach snaps to the bias strip and snap collar onto vest. Trim loose fiber ends as desired.

6. Sew on decorative beads as desired.

For the Strip-Woven Felted Collar

1. Dye assorted discarded knit items, such as wool socks or sweaters, according to package instructions. This helps visually blend the different colors of the recycled knits.

2. Cut the dyed knit items into strips.

3. Pin-weave knit strips with lengths of unspun wool (also called roving) in a basic over-under fashion, to create a loosely woven length. Insert bits of curly mohair or other fibers for color and texture, as desired.

4. Baste the woven length of wool between two layers of muslin.

5. Put the wool-muslin "sandwich" through at least two long washing machine cycles, set on the most vigorous agitation, then dry in a hot dryer. This will cause the wool to felt.

6. Remove basting and muslin; cut the collar pattern from the felted wool and assemble collar.

Tips from the designer

■ For the greatest efficiency, use an even number of snaps and alternate the male and female halves around the neckline. For example, use four snap sets, and alternate them male-female around the neckline of the vest. Then, you will need only four snap sets for any detachable collar you make, alternating the male and female halves to fit the snaps along the vest neckline.

■ Because a collar covers a fairly small area, you can indulge in exotic fabrics, complex surface treatments, or dramatic color combinations without risking an entire garment. Yet, because it's placed near the face, a collar can be as attention-getting and interesting as unusual jewelry.

■ Pintucking a sheer metallic fabric is lots of fun. It glitters in the light and the colored threads inside the pintucks provide extra interest.

Plan for the Week

Monday
〜〜〜
Tuesday
〜〜〜
Wednesday
〜〜〜
Thursday
Pretreat collar fabrics; select completed vest.
Friday
Make collar pattern; manipulate pattern to achieve desired collar shape and size.
Saturday
Cut out collar; begin collar construction.
Sunday
Complete collar construction and attach to vest.

When you're short on time, simplicity is a requirement. In this classic vest, the loosely-woven tweed is easily fringed for a custom matching trim.

Design and construction details

The designer sought to create a distinctive garment while controlling the time and money expended on it.

■ She did not line the vest because the fabric has enough body to be unsupported. To cover interior construction details, she bound the seam allowances with a sheer seam finishing tape and used a peach taffeta for narrow facings around the armholes and along the front and hem edges.

■ Instead of making a buttonhole in the loosely-woven fabric, she constructed a fringed rectangle as the "closure" and sewed a button on top. A nylon snap hidden underneath does the actual fastening.

■ She took advantage of the fabric's different warp and weft colors in the fringed trim. When the fabric is unraveled from the crosswise direction, the fringe is a mottled gray; from the lengthwise direction, it is peach, light gray, off-white, and caramel. Narrow strips of fabric fringed in each colorway decorate the upper left shoulder and extend away from the vest closure.

Bouquet of Color
DESIGNER
Pat Scheible

Fashion a colorful tableau of favorite fabrics and blend them all together with a multicolor madras.

Design and construction details

The designer had some leftover scraps of handmade fabrics by North Carolina weaver Fran Gardner that she wanted to incorporate into a new garment; the scraps were too pretty to toss.

■ She cut the jacket pattern pieces from different small pieces, depending on the size and shape of the scraps, and assembled the jacket according to pattern instructions.

■ To pull the fabric assortment together, she made bias tape and piping from the same cotton madras that lines the jacket, topstitching the bias tape in place over the construction seams before inserting the lining.

■ For a surprising detail and nice touch of color, she also used the madras for the "lips" of the bound buttonholes.

Tips from the designer

■ Madras is great for unifying different fabrics. It comes in a wide variety of multicolor plaids and the fact that the warp and weft are different colors adds to its blending power. It's also a perfect weight for bias tape.

THE MADRAS LINING FABRIC IS PERFECT FOR CUSTOM BIAS TAPE THAT COVERS THE CONSTRUCTION SEAMS AND BLENDS THE ASSORTED HANDWOVEN FABRICS INTO A UNIFIED COLOR PALETTE. IT ALSO MAKES A PRETTY MULTICOLOR PIPING AND ADDS BRIGHT SPOTS OF COLOR TO THE BOUND BUTTONHOLES.

Sew up a quick sweater jacket pattern in fleece, for cozy comfort and warmth. This print is cut on the bias to create an interesting chevron design.

Design and construction details

The designer converted a pullover style to a front-closing sweater jacket and then used the fabric's unique qualities to make other refinements.

■ She cut the jacket on the bias, to take advantage of the fabric's linear design. This resulted in a flattering chevron design that leads the eye up and away from the hipline, creating a slimming effect.

■ The placket, which is cut on the fabric's straight grain, stabilizes the bias-cut front pieces and keeps the jacket from stretching out of shape.

■ To add a tailored finishing touch, she made faux bound buttonholes in the completed garment, which is so easy to do in this non-raveling fleece. Cut a 2½" (6.5 cm) square of self-fabric for each buttonhole; pin each square in place, right sides together, and stitch a small rectangle that is long enough for the selected buttons (see illustration). Slash along center of rectangle and into corners, and turn fabric square to inside; edgestitch around opening. On inside of garment, fold back excess fabric on each long side of buttonhole and butt folds along center of rectangle to form faux welts. Pin in place and stitch around the rectangle ⅛ ¼" (3 6 mm) from opening. Trim excess fabric close to stitching.

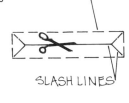

STITCHING LINE

SLASH LINES

Tips from the designer

■ When sewing with fleece, use a ballpoint sewing machine needle and increase the stitch length a bit. And never press fleece, because you will melt the fabric.

■ Look for interesting design options in different fleece patterns. In the jacket shown here, I centered each buttonhole on a repeating design motif so that each button would be nicely framed.

Style Of A Different Stripe
DESIGNER
M. Luanne Carson

A traditional jacket lapel certainly doesn't have to be conventional or boring as this inventive striped design proves.

Design details

The designer adapted a conservative jacket pattern for creative expression, without compromising its classy distinction.

■ She used both sides of the fabric in different areas of the garment, to inventively contrast dark and light.

■ She incorporated strips of sandwashed rayon into the lapel construction, in a color that echoes the red pinstripes of the fashion fabric. The strips also break up the overall darkness of the jacket and create an attention-getting frame for the wearer's face.

■ The bias cuffs and piping add yet another interesting element, by subtly contrasting the diagonal lines of the bias with the vertical stripes of the jacket body.

Tips from the designer

■ In some fabrics, there is no such thing as "right" and "wrong" sides. Both can be used to create visual interest, so don't be afraid to let the wrong side show.

■ By playing around with contrast, between colors or stripe directions, you can easily turn a very simple garment design into a compliment-getting original. And you don't even have to alter the pattern!

Vest Deco
DESIGNER
Mary Russell

This versatile style is a colorful accent piece for everything from casual jeans to a black velvet dress.

Materials and supplies

■ Pattern for vest with collar, or simple jacket (sleeves will be omitted)

■ Fabric of choice for vest and contrasting collar

■ Lining fabric, as required by pattern

■ Assorted fabric scraps for patchwork

■ Interfacing for collar

■ Thread to match vest fabric

■ Invisible thread to machine appliqué patchwork to collar

■ Cutting supplies, or rotary cutter and mat

■ Notions required by pattern

■ Zippers (optional)

Construction details

1. Cut the collar and collar interfacing slightly larger than the pattern pieces. Cut all other pieces to actual pattern size.

2. Assemble patchwork units for collar detail. The vest shown here uses a Double Wedding Ring pattern.

3. Interface collar.

4. Lay patchwork on collar in the desired position. Machine-stitch in place, using invisible thread.

5. Trim collar to size of pattern piece.

6. Assemble vest according to pattern directions.

"Collars are a great place to give a garment unique flair. A touch of patchwork, embroidery, or appliqué quickly and easily turns a simple style into a one-of-a-kind piece."

Tips from the designer

■ Instead of searching for a vest pattern with a collar, use a simple jacket pattern and omit the sleeves. This takes a lot less time than drafting a new collar to fit a specific vest pattern.

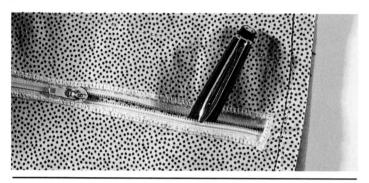

THE DESIGNER INCORPORATED HIDDEN ZIPPERED POCKETS ON THE INSIDE OF THE VEST BY INSERTING THEM INTO THE LINING SO NO STITCHING WOULD SHOW ON THE OUTSIDE.

Plan for the Week

Monday

∽∽∽

Tuesday

∽∽∽

Wednesday

Pretreat fabrics.

Thursday

Lay out, cut, and mark vest and lining; interface appropriate pieces (interface collar later).

Friday

Install zippered pockets in lining, if desired.

Saturday

Assemble and attach patchwork for collar; complete collar construction.

Sunday

Complete vest construction.

Laotian Jacket
DESIGNER
Pat Scheible

Design and construction details

The designer didn't want to mutilate the yardage she bought in Laos by cutting into it, so she devised this variation on a cocoon jacket. The length of silk is handwoven for the "sin," a traditional Laotian wrap skirt, and it includes a coordinating border.

■ To form the jacket, the designer folded the lower corners up to the opposite long edge, to form sleeves. See Figure 1. She used standing French seams along the shoulder.

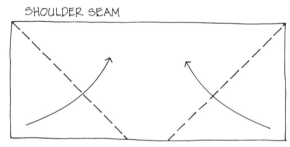

FIG. 1 FORMING SLEEVES

■ To shape the upper back, she pleated the neck edge and basted it in place before attaching the band. See Figure 2.

■ For the sleeves, she cut off the tips of the triangles to make sleeve openings, and gathered the openings to fit her wrists.

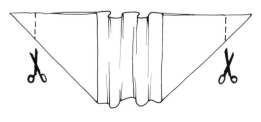

FIG. 2 PLEATING NECKLINE

This simple cocoon-style jacket shows off the beautiful handwoven silk yardage, and uses the fabric's border for a perfectly coordinated trim.

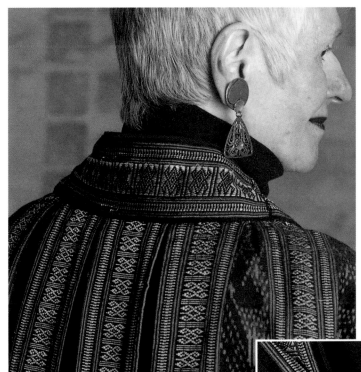

TO SHAPE THE JACKET'S UPPER BACK SO IT CURVES OVER THE BODY, THE DESIGNER PLEATED THE NECKLINE'S STRAIGHT EDGE BEFORE ATTACHING IT TO THE BAND.

■ To finish the jacket, the designer made a piped and faced band from the border fabric, which she used for cuffs and a front band.

■ For a special finishing touch, she mitered the ends of the front bands and added tassels, just for fun.

THE FABRIC'S BORDER MAKES A BEAUTIFUL FRONT BAND ON THIS COCOON-STYLE JACKET, AND THE TASSELS ADD A FUN FINISHING TOUCH.

Vest With Two Faces
DESIGNER
Karen Swing

Show off your machine quilting experiments in this easy-to-sew reversible style.

Materials and supplies

- Pattern for simple vest with no darts

- Fashion fabric, as required by pattern

- Complementary lining fabric, in amount equal to fashion fabric

- ¼ yard (.25 m) coordinating or contrasting fabric for binding edges (or use fashion or lining fabric)

- Flannel or thin polyester quilt batting, in amount equal to fashion fabric

- Thread in coordinating or contrasting colors

- Sewing machine with darning or embroidery foot

- Notions required by pattern

Construction details

1. Cut out fashion fabric, lining, and flannel or batting, according to pattern layouts. If you are using one of the main fabrics for the binding, reserve ¼ yard (.25 m).

2. Cut off seam allowances of all outside edges, including front, neckline, and hem. Do not remove seam allowances for side or shoulder seams. If the pattern calls for binding to finish the edges, do not remove any seam allowances.

3. Pin left front, right front, and back layers together with the main fabric on top, batting or flannel in the middle, and lining fabric on the bottom, to create a sandwich effect. All layers should be smooth and wrinkle-free, to prevent tucks while quilting.

4. Machine quilt layered pieces in an overall, densely stitched pattern. Whenever possible, start a new line of stitching from an outside edge, to prevent knots in the center of the piece.

5. After quilting a little bit, put the needle down through the fabric and check the back side to see that the stitches are well-balanced. You may need to adjust the top tension.

6. Continue quilting, spreading your fingers as though they were an embroidery hoop to gently pull the fabric away from the needle in all directions as you stitch.

7. When the quilting is complete, choose the side on which you want the seam finish to show. If your binding fabric matches the vest fabric, the bound edges will virtually disappear; if it contrasts with the vest fabric, the bound edge will become a design element.

8. Complete vest construction and bind all edges with selected fabric.

Tips from the designer

■ Gently pull on the binding as you sew it around the front, neckline, and armhole curves. This urges the binding to conform to the shape of the vest.

■ If you run out of bobbin thread and must begin quilting in the center of a piece, put the needle down into the fabric and then back up, while holding the tail of the needle thread. Then pull the needle thread upward, to draw the bobbin thread up through the fabric to the top. Knot the threads by stitching for about ¼" (6 mm) in very small stitches. Do not sew in place, as this will produce a wad of thread that is unsightly and may eventually become undone. Use the same technique to end quilting if you must stop in the middle of the piece.

■ If you want the front to close, but don't want to use buttonholes on a reversible vest, simply replace them with one set of button loops and two different sets of buttons.

Plan for the Week

Monday

Tuesday

Wednesday
Pretreat fabrics.
Thursday
Lay out, cut, and mark vest pattern from fashion fabric, lining, and flannel or batting.
Friday
Pin fabric layers together; experiment with quilting technique on scraps.
Saturday
Machine quilt vest pieces.
Sunday
Complete vest construction; bind edges.

Keepsake Jacket
DESIGNER
Ann E. Beck

Create a wearable treasure of favorite fabric swatches, laces, ribbons, threads, buttons, and beads with this easy four-layer approach to jacket construction.

Materials and supplies

- Unstructured jacket pattern of choice, preferably one without collar or tailored details

- Muslin, to equal yardage required by pattern

- Lining fabric, as required by pattern

- Assorted fabric scraps, to equal yardage required by pattern

- Lightweight fusible interfacing

- Rayon and/or metallic machine embroidery thread

- Assorted decorative threads, yards, and cording

- Assorted trims and embellishments

- Rubber bands

- Machine embroidery needles and accessories

- Notions required by pattern

Construction details

1. Cut the jacket fronts, back, and sleeves out of the muslin, adding ½-1" (1.25-2.5 cm) around outer edges of all pieces.

2. Manipulate some of the assorted fabric scraps to achieve interesting textures. The designer used a fabric fringe, made from 1" (2.5 cm) strips of assorted fabrics; she also textured the fabric with intentional wrinkling. To wrinkle, thoroughly wet a fabric piece and wring out. Fold the piece into a long strip, twist into a tube, and roll up into a compact ball; secure with rubber bands. Dry in a clothes dryer. Remove rubber bands and open up fabric; to preserve wrinkles, fuse lightweight interfacing to wrong side.

3. For the first layer, cover the muslin pieces with pieced arrangements of plain and manipulated fabric scraps. Stitch the first scrap to the muslin foundation; stitch the second scrap to the first, right sides together; flip open and press flat. Repeat with other scraps, stitching each one to the previous one, until the muslin foundation pieces are completely covered.

4. For the second layer, embellish pieced arrangements with decorative machine stitching, using colored or metallic threads and various stitches.

5. For the third layer, couch decorative yarns and cords to the surface, using colored or metallic threads and various stitches.

6. For the fourth "finishing touch" layer, arrange embellishments such as beads, buttons, and bits of lace or ribbon and hand stitch them to the surface.

7. Compare embellished vest components to pattern pieces; trim excess fabric around outer edges to pattern cutting lines.

8. Assemble and line jacket, according to pattern instructions.

Tips from the designer

- It's really easy to go overboard with this layered technique, because we all accumulate so many wonderful scraps and embellishments over the years. A little restraint is a good thing; try to balance color, texture, and complexity of the overall design.

- If you're short on time, make the jacket back in plain unembellished fabric and get fancy just on the fronts.

- It helps to experiment with different machine embroidery stitches and threads ahead of time. You'll learn how to set up the machine and what decorative results you can expect.

Plan for the Week

Monday
Pretreat fabrics and manipulate some swatches, if desired; experiment with machine embroidery stitches and threads.

Tuesday
Cut out muslin vest; experiment with arrangements of fabric scraps.

Wednesday
Finalize fabric arrangements and stitch to muslin foundation pieces.

Thursday
Complete machine embroidery on fabric arrangements.

Friday
Couch decorative threads and cords onto surface.

Saturday
Add buttons, trims, and other embellishments; begin jacket construction.

Sunday
Complete jacket construction.

Celestial Vest

DESIGNER
Karen M. Bennett

The stars will shine upon you and the company you keep when you wear this heavenly reversible vest.

Materials and supplies

- Pattern for bolero-style vest with no darts
- Fashion fabric of choice, in amount required by pattern
- Lining fabric, as required by pattern
- Muslin, to equal fashion fabric yardage
- ⅓ yard (.3 m) accent fabric of choice
- ½ yard (.5 m) coordinating or contrasting fabric for piping
- Length of cording, in amount equal to outer edges of vest
- Fusible web product
- Metallic thread and appropriate sewing machine needle
- Sewing thread to coordinate with fashion fabric
- Machine darning or quilting foot
- Stabilizer
- Notions required by pattern

Construction details

1. Trace the left and right vest front and vest back pattern pieces on the fashion fabric. Do not cut them out until the quilting is completed.

2. Place the muslin underneath the fashion fabric, right side up; pin securely at regular intervals through both layers.

3. Apply fusible web to wrong side of the accent fabric, according to manufacturer's directions, and cut out desired appliqué shapes.

4. Arrange shapes on the traced vest fronts and back, as desired, and fuse them into place.

5. To machine quilt the layered fabric and muslin, drop the sewing machine feed dogs and attach a darning or quilting foot. Reduce the bobbin tension and stitch at a medium speed with the metallic thread, controlling the length of the stitches as you move the fabric back and forth. Try making loops or waves across the fabric, but do not cross over any threads you have already sewn. As you come to the appliqué shapes, be sure to stitch down the centers and all points, to hold them in place.

6. Press the quilted fabric and cut out the vest pattern pieces; sew shoulder seams.

7. To make piping, cover cording with desired fabric and baste to outer edges of vest along seamlines.

8. Cut out and position one large star at center back of the back lining piece and smaller stars on left and right front lining pieces. Place stabilizer underneath lining fabric and stitch star shapes in place.

9. Sew lining shoulder seams.

10. Complete vest construction, according to pattern directions.

Tips from the designer

- Relax and have fun with the machine quilting. Loosen up your arms and shoulders before you start; if you are tight and tense, your stitching will be, too.

- You will quickly get comfortable with controlling the speed and motion of the machine quilting, and may even feel so adept that you'll want to sign the vest during the quilting process.

- A narrow piping along the outside edges adds a subtle design contrast and a sleek finish.

ONCE YOU FEEL COMFORTABLE WITH CONTROLLING THE SPEED AND
MOTION OF THE MACHINE QUILTING, YOU CAN ADD YOUR SIGNATURE TO
THE DESIGN.

Plan for the Week

Monday

〜〜〜〜

Tuesday
Pretreat fabrics.

Wednesday
Trace vest fronts and back on fashion fabric; pin to muslin.

Thursday
Cut out appliqué shapes and fuse to fashion fabric.

Friday
Machine quilt layered fashion fabric and muslin; cut out vest fronts and back.

Saturday
Make piping and baste to vest pieces; cut out star appliqués and apply to lining pieces.

Sunday
Complete vest construction.

Strip-Woven Style
DESIGNER
Jean Davidson

This simple finger-weaving technique offers a great opportunity to recycle fabrics or experiment with color and texture.

Materials and supplies

- Pattern for simple vest with no darts

- Three different fabrics, to equal yardage required by pattern, in coordinating or contrasting colors: one marked A and one marked B to be cut in 1¼" (3 cm) bias strips, and a third for the foundation or base fabric, which becomes the vest lining (solid color is recommended for a first project)

- Thread in coordinating color for all three fabrics

- 45-degree triangle

- Rotary cutter and mat, or cutting supplies

- Sewing machine with zigzag or assorted decorative stitches

- Large supply of straight pins

- Notions required by pattern

Construction details

1. Cut out base fabric according to pattern layout.

2. Using 45-degree triangle as a guide, cut all of fabrics A and B in 1¼" (3 cm) bias strips.

3. Place right and left front base pieces on a flat surface, wrong side up. Use triangle and pencil to mark diagonal guidelines the width of each bias strip on each front piece.

4. Cover entire surface of front base pieces with fabric A strips, taking care to keep them within the diagonal guidelines.

5. Weave fabric B strips in and out of, and at diagonal opposites to, fabric A strips. Pin in place (this takes a lot of pins!).

6. Lay back base piece down on flat surface and repeat the marking, weaving, and pinning process.

7. Select a decorative or wide zigzag machine stitch. Start at the center of each garment piece and stitch along the center of each bias strip in both directions. Remove pins as you sew.

8. Assemble the garment according to pattern instructions.

9. With remaining bias strips, self-bind all raw edges for a neat finish.

Tips from the designer

■ If you haven't used a rotary cutter, now is the time to try. It really speeds up the task of cutting bias strips. To protect your cutting surface, use a self-healing mat.

■ After practicing the basic technique in a first vest, experiment with multiple-color weavings and/or print variations.

■ When the vest is completed, launder it frequently so the texture of the raw-edged woven strips will get more interesting. Don't worry, the bias-cut fabric strips won't ravel too much.

Plan for the Week

Monday

Tuesday
Pretreat fabrics.

Wednesday
Lay out, cut, and mark **vest base** or foundation fabric.

Thursday
Cut bias strips.

Friday
Weave and pin strips to base pieces.

Saturday
Stitch woven strips in place; begin vest construction.

Sunday
Complete vest construction; bind edges.

Mountain Landscape

DESIGNER

Penny Grace

Sewing disasters can become wardrobe favorites, such as this elegant vest that salvages a heart-breaking mistake.

Design and construction details

The designer started with an unsuccessful silk-painting project: a hand-painted winter landscape in gray dyes tinted with other colors to give some variation in tone. But when the silk emerged from the steam-fixing process, it had acquired an overall yellowish tone. She decided to "get the yellow out" with a bit of bleach, but the silk yellowed even more and the fabric frayed badly as well.

Disgusted, she tossed the project into a corner until a life-saving idea evolved. The fabric's frayed edges eventually attracted the designer and she decided to cut the silk up and assemble a landscape collage on a completed vest.

■ She applied fusible stabilizer to the wrong side of the silk, cut out landscape shapes, and applied them to the vest. For decorative interest, she stitched them in place with free-motion machine embroidery.

■ She chose a burgundy silk lining fabric to pick up the rose-colored areas of the landscape and also contrast with the more subtle tones of the design.

■ For finishing touches, she selected bone buttons that complement the natural look of the vest.

Tips from the designer

■ While you can make this type of vest in a weekend, some of the components may sit in a corner of your sewing room for months! But you don't have to go to such extremes. Simply find a fabric that suggests a landscape theme and evaluate how you can cut it into interesting appliqué shapes.

■ Be sure the vest fabric is compatible with the landscape fabric, so you can incorporate it into the overall design.

■ Don't be afraid to re-cut the shapes, move them to different spots, or even eliminate some. Rearrange them until you achieve a design to your liking.

■ For the best results, apply a fusible backing to the appliqué shapes and fuse them to the cut-out vest pieces before stitching in place. Then, use a tear-away stabilizer underneath the vest pieces when stitching the appliqués, to provide support and give a smooth finish.

FOR A SPECIAL TOUCH, APPLY SOME OF THE EXTRA SHAPES TO THE INSIDE LINING. THE FINISHED VEST BECOMES A WORK OF ART, BOTH INSIDE AND OUT.

CREATING A MASTERPIECE FROM NOTHING
(or Almost Nothing)

By Penny Grace

I feel so satisfied when I can recycle a mistake into a masterpiece, or transform scraps that have been piling up into something beautiful. Most of my vests are created this way. I prefer using good quality wool or cotton for the vest fabric and hand-painted silk for the appliqués.

The most time-consuming part is creating the design, from the initial idea or sketch to choosing the fabrics to cutting and placing the shapes on the vest. You might want to start this process early in the week, perhaps doing a little each night.

When the family is busy with video games or comfortably ensconced in front of the football game on television, make your move! Announce in a suitably serious tone of voice that you have important work to do and are not to be disturbed.

Make yourself a pot of coffee or pour a glass of wine, and take it to your workroom, bedroom, dining room, or wherever you work. Close the door behind you, if you can. Spread out your scraps or sewing "mistakes" and look for pieces that will work together and with your selected vest fabric. Motifs or patterns in the fabrics may suggest an overall design theme, such as trees, flowers, geometrics, or other shapes.

Arrange and rearrange the shapes on the vest pieces until you're satisfied with the design, and lightly fuse them into place (cover with a pressing sheet suitable for use with appliqué). When cool the fused pieces can be gently pulled up and repositioned. However, don't overdo this, as you will lose some of the fabric's freshness, especially if it frays easily.

Once you have the design to your liking, stop! Stand back and admire your masterpiece. Give yourself a pat on the back, make a toast to your artistry, and then proceed to stitch the design in place.

By now, the family is probably wondering where you are and what's for dinner (order in pizza). You can now rejoin your family secure in the knowledge that you have just completed a Herculean task: making something beautiful from almost nothing at all.

Terry With A Twist
DESIGNER
Fradele Feld

How many towels can you possibly use in the bathroom? Instead use some of these beautiful terry cloth designs for creative new fashions.

Design and construction details

The designer started with a simple jacket pattern that already had insets and smaller sections in it; she further subdivided the pattern pieces to take advantage of the designs in her terry cloth towels and create the final mosaic effect.

■ She first evaluated the jacket pattern to determine which sections would look good in the main color, and which in pieced terry cloth or other coordinating fabrics. She further subdivided the pattern into smaller sections to accommodate the various prints and patterns of the assorted fabrics.

■ She made some sketches of the jacket silhouette in different combinations of the towel patterns and base fabric, until she arrived at an overall effect she liked.

■ Based on her sketches, she cut the design components out of the terry cloth and other fabrics, and pieced them together during the jacket's construction.

■ The designer loves hats, so she used the jacket's leftover scraps to fashion a fun coordinating accessory. She started with a simple hat pattern, cut the pattern pieces into smaller sections, and added seam allowances, just as she did for the jacket.

Tips from the designer

■ You can easily divide any pattern into sections for interesting pieced fabric effects, but you might not want to cut your original pattern apart. Instead, just trace the pattern pieces on pattern-making paper, tissue paper, or any other tracing product. Then, you can cut and split the traced version to your heart's content, leaving your original pattern intact. Don't forget to add seam allowances to all split or newly cut edges.

■ If you are uncomfortable with sketching various design combinations, just enlarge the line drawing on the pattern envelope and make several copies. Then, you can use the copies to draw various design options for your garment.

■ Experiment with both symmetrical and asymmetrical designs. The results are radically different, yet can be equally interesting.

■ If the towels you use are very colorful or ornate, you might want to balance them with larger sections of the main color or fewer areas of other fabrics. Too much pattern can clash and look busy.

■ If your towels tend to unravel when cut, serge the cut edges and plan ahead for ¾" (2 cm) seam allowances.

■ Making buttonholes in terry cloth can be a pain. Instead, use button loops or close your jacket with a dramatic, yet complementary, pin.

Spotlight On Trim
DESIGNER
Sallie Rae Ruff

Dig into your stash of favorite trims and decorative threads for this wearable showcase of color and texture.

Materials and supplies

- Favorite lined vest pattern, preferably one without darts
- Fashion fabric and lining, as required by pattern
- Assorted cords, braids, and textured yarns to coordinate with colors in fashion fabric
- Store-bought or custom piping to coordinate with fabric
- Zipper foot
- Notions required by pattern

Construction details

1. Cut vest pattern out of fashion fabric and lining. Set lining pieces aside.

2. Arrange varying lengths of braid, cords, and yarns on vest fronts and back; stitch in place with decorative machine stitches or wide zigzag. Use matching or contrasting thread, as desired. Stitch trims to vest in a random as-you-go fashion, or determine placement ahead of time and pin decorative elements in place before stitching.

3. When decorative braid and yarns are stitched in place, construct and line vest according to pattern instructions.

4. For piped edges, baste piping along seamline of vest fabric before stitching fabric and lining together; use zipper foot when stitching piping.

Tips from the designer

- Using a fabric's interesting pattern as a starting point for applied embellishments is a fun and easy way to spiff up a simple garment. This vest dresses up a black knit dress beautifully, and also looks great with casual jeans and T-shirt.

- Stitch the wider, fatter braids or yarns down first, and then let the thinner, more delicate strands meander around and on top of them.

Gold Star Vest
DESIGNER
Vicki Gadberry

Stars and stripes go together in this easy-to-make reversible vest that's also a great showcase for a wonderful assortment of fabrics.

Design details

On a recent trip to the fabric store, a selection of star-printed materials caught the designer's eye. She purchased small amounts of several different types and then selected coordinating prints from her fabric stash to go together in this theme vest. She strip pieced custom cloth for both the vest inside and outside, added button loops in the front opening seam, and sewed buttons on both sides for a reversible fashion. For a nice surprise, she used a single half-moon button among the gold stars.

Jigsaw Puzzle Jacket
DESIGNER
Barbara Fugazzotto

Interesting shapes of related fabrics fit together like puzzle pieces in this attractive asymmetrical jacket design.

Design and construction details

The designer started with a pattern for a traditional Chinese jacket, but altered the shape of the pattern for a less boxy contour. She then created a jigsaw puzzle of various related fabrics and textures and stitched the collage to a base fabric.

■ For a more dolman style at the shoulder and tapered silhouette at the wrist, the designer redrew the lines of the pattern. See Figure 1.

■ She then redrew the jewel neckline on one side to form the asymmetrical shape; the other side is folded back like a lapel. See Figure 2. The altered pattern was cut out of a muslin base fabric.

■ For the "puzzle pieces," the designer cut freeform shapes from upholstery fabrics and laid them down on the muslin pattern, overlapping the edges slightly. The shapes were arranged and rearranged until she was satisfied and the muslin pieces were completely covered.

■ She serged around the edges of the shapes one by one, and pinned them back in place on the muslin. Then, she zigzagged the appliqué composition to the muslin base fabric.

■ The finished pieces were stay stitched around the edges before assembling and lining the jacket. An attractively fringed selvage was stitched into the shoulder seam for its textural effect, and the hem and opening edges were bound with a coordinating fabric.

Tips from the designer

■ For an asymmetrical neckline, draw some ideas on paper first. Then cut them out and hold them up to your neckline area and see what you think.

■ For the puzzle piece collage, cut shapes in large, medium, and small sizes for visual interest. And make the shapes somewhat related, such as all angular or all curvy. Too much variety can result in a disorganized look.

■ When arranging your appliqué shapes on the garment pieces, try to keep the whole composition in mind: front to back and side to side. Lay the two fronts next to each other and plan the design of each side to work well with the other; consider how the front design will transition to the back.

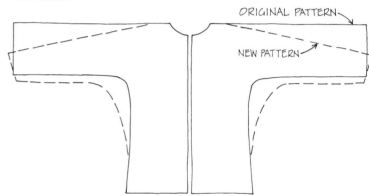

Figure 1. The designer redrew the original pattern's shape for sleeves that are not quite as boxy as the original and that taper toward the wrist.

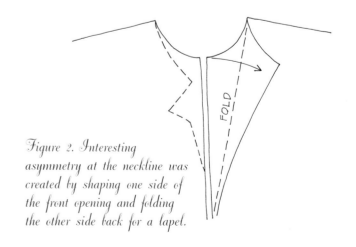

Figure 2. Interesting asymmetry at the neckline was created by shaping one side of the front opening and folding the other side back for a lapel.

Joyce Baldwin

is Assistant Professor of Textiles at Western Carolina University in Cullowhee, North Carolina. She passes on her love of fabrics and fashion design to classrooms full of students, and plans periodic student trips to the New York City fashion centers, where she also manages to shop for sewing supplies for her own studio.

Ann E. Beck

is a self-taught fiber artist who has been sewing wearable art for several years; she also sells her work at craft shows and by private commissions. She works full time as a CPA for a multi-national company and has three small children. She lives in St. Petersburg, Florida, where you will find her sewing in the wee hours of the morning.

Karen M. Bennett

lives in Alexander, North Carolina, and has been a member of the Southern Highland Craft Guild since 1983. An energetic woman, she home schools her four children, keeps a large organic garden, sells her tatting, embroidery, and sewing in galleries and shops, and teaches classes for the local chapter of the Embroiderer's Guild of America. A career highlight was the 1993 commission of a tatted angel for the White House Christmas tree.

Sheila Bennitt

recently relocated to Asheville, North Carolina from Texas, where she sold fanciful fashions from her design studio. She is also a painter and sees many parallels in design and technique between working with fabric and paint.

M. Luanne Carson

thrives on the creative process of integrating fabric and style for unusual effect. She combines her formal training in clothing and textiles with her success as an educator to excite her students about their creative potential. Even after many years at the machine, sewing continues to galvanize Luanne's thoughts and activities. She lives in Arden, North Carolina.

Jean Davidson

is a landscape architect, by profession, and sews for her own pleasure in Aptos, California. She says that sewing has been a common thread throughout her life and she always looks for new stitching tangents to explore, such as tucking, smocking, quiltmaking, mola appliqué, and weaving. Recently, she has been teaching her granddaughter to sew.

Fradele Feld

has been designing clothes since outfitting her paper dolls as a little girl. She has degrees in fashion design and education, and is active in the Embroiderer's Guild of America, as well as other quilting and embroidery guilds. Her first love is clothing that allows her to experiment with boldly patterned fabrics and new ways of combining and embellishing them. Fradele lives in Cherry Hill, New Jersey.

Barbara Fugazzotto

says that her early childhood experience with fabrics, yarns, and handwork of all types has matured into a love for designing unique clothing. She particularly enjoys the artful combination of individual units into larger compositions. Her mixed media and fabric art works have been represented widely in exhibitions and galleries. Barbara lives in Jensen Beach, Florida.

Vicki Gadberry

recently moved to Ft. Davis, Texas, where she watches deer, antelope, and wild turkey wander past her house. She also weaves, sews, and works as a carpenter's helper, librarian, and office assistant for a crafts importing business. She recently completed some independent research on Black Mountain College, the Bauhaus, and WPA art programs.

Penny Grace

thinks of her appliqué designs as huge jigsaw puzzles, putting scraps of hand-painted silk together in new and different ways to create unique clothing. She lives in Kitchener, Ontario.

Aileen S. Gugenheim

has been sewing and designing since childhood, and "discovered" wearable art 25 years ago. She also has a degree in fine art and is the owner of Design Specialties, a home-based art-to-wear design firm in Houston, Texas. In addition to working with fabric, she designs button necklaces; her work can be seen in The Button Craft Book, by Dawn Cusick (Lark Books).

Sonia A. Huber

says that taking classes in pattern drafting, after many years of sewing, opened up a new world for her. She has found that time is short for everyone, so making simple changes to a favorite pattern can take it from the realm of "off the rack" to out of the ordinary.

Elma Johnson

is a multi-talented artist who works in ceramics, brick, glass, paper, and textiles. She recently retired from the University of North Carolina, Asheville, where she taught most of these skills. A new direction has been experimenting with a knitting machine to create custom yardage.

Beth Karjala

uses surface embellishment to add texture and produce a three-dimensional quality that captures the drama of fashion. She says her personal style evolved from a desire to create a visual vocabulary of movement with the flow of the design or dangling embellishments. Beth lives in Marine on St. Croix, Minnesota.

Mary S. Cissell Lucas

learned to weave in Germany about fifteen years ago and had to sharpen her sewing skills in order to work with her handwoven cloth. She is currently learning ceramics, and intends to combine clay and fibers in a new form of basketry. Mary lives in Waynesville, North Carolina.

Lisa Mandle

is the owner and principal designer of Only One, a custom one-of-a-kind clothing and accessories business in Marshall, North Carolina. She has had extensive experience in the fashion and costume design fields, and was selected in 1984 as one of the top ten designers in Washington, D.C. In her current business, she emphasizes the unique qualities of clothing and never makes a design from the collection the same way twice, hence the name, Only One.

Thelma P. Matthews

took early retirement from a career in software support with IBM and used her free time to develop and expand her expertise in designing and making formal dresses. She has recently become fascinated with silk painting, weaving, and quilting. She lives in Tampa, Florida.

Mary S. Parker

is descended from a long line of quilters and seamstresses. Her love of sewing and a fondness for cats have remained constant throughout a changing array of professional career positions. Mary lives in Asheville, North Carolina, and recently moved into a larger house with her understanding husband so that she would have sufficient room for her growing fabric stash.

Judith S. Plucker

is a versatile commercial designer and artist who lives in Afton, Tennessee. Her work spans a 30-year career designing gift wrap, packaging, and cards for clients such as Hallmark, Russell Stover Candies, and American Greetings. She also designs clothing and theater costumes and sets. Judith is an accomplished watercolorist and particularly loves painting the native flora of Tennessee.

Charlotte Redemann

has been sewing for more than 20 years and finds that fabric provides inspiration for many types of pieces, including clothing and other textile art works. She firmly believes that original fashions need to be flattering to the wearer, instead of just using the human body as a display surface for different fabric techniques. Charlotte lives in Montgomery, Alabama.

Margaret Richardson

learned to sew many years ago, when home economics was still part of the school curriculum. She is concerned about the declining number of people who sew and does her part to support her local fabric and quilting shops in Tacoma, Washington. Margaret is also active as a lecturer, volunteer, and participant at various annual costume events and conventions.

Judith Robertson

has been sewing since she was eight years old, and loves the challenge of making something that is distinctly her own. Because she is not too keen on frequent shopping, she enjoys using things that are already on hand, such as scraps of fabric, to add a twist to simple, time-tested designs.

Piper Hubbell Robinson

operates a one-of-a-kind garment design studio called Wear For Art Thou in Elmhurst, Illinois. She draws on her many years of classical ballet and her formal training in fashion design to interpret line, shape, form, and movement in fabric. Piper says the process of creating garments is completed by the act of wearing them.

Sallie Rae Ruff

started sewing when she was twelve years old, and won her first sewing contest when she was fourteen. With an Associate Arts degree in Fashion Merchandising, Sallie has always dreamed of becoming a designer. She loves machine appliqué and uses it to give her custom "contemporary country" garments an individual touch.

Mary Russell

is a quilt artist living in San Luis Obispo, California. Her wearable quilt art has been featured in various fashion shows and publications. She also is the maker of Double Wedding Ring Rulers, which eliminate the need to trace templates when cutting patches for that quilt pattern.

Joneen M. Sargent

likes the creative outlet that sewing provides and loves to try new things. She started sewing back in high school and makes quilts and clothing for herself and her family. Joneen lives in Bristol, Tennessee.

Pat Scheible

is a decorative painter by trade. She designs and creates with fiber, paint, and most any other material that strikes her fancy. Pat lives in Mebane, North Carolina.

Elizabeth Searle

started sewing in the crib, according to her grandmother. She has a dressmaking business in Asheville, North Carolina, teaches creative sewing techniques in area classes, and still has time to experiment with creative art-to-wear clothing for herself and her clients.

Karen Swing

has been sewing since she was twelve years old and is now a full-time fabric artist in Boone, North Carolina. She makes art quilts, but her first love is one-of-a-kind wearables. Karen has been particularly enjoying machine embroidery and experimenting with the different effects of dyeing.

ACKNOWLEDGMENTS

The behind-the-scenes support system of designers, photographers, models, friends, and others is indispensable to every author. No book would get done without these creative and generous folks, and my sincere thanks go to all of them:

■ **the designers**, whose creativity, ingenuity, enthusiasm, and sewing energy are truly inspiring.

■ **the models**, who graciously took time away from their real life occupations to dress up for the camera: Beth Benischek, Paige Blomgren, Naomi Brown, M. Luanne Carson, Jessi Cinque, Linda Constable, Diana DeNardis, Sharon DeYoung, Katie DuMont, Christina Faulk, Susan Fisher, Karen Gettinger, Erran Gilchrist, Gwendolyn Marvels, Marion Mathews, Celia Naranjo, Micah Pulleyn, Sandra Soto, Nicole Tuggle, and Juanita Wright.

■ **Richard Babb**, who is a true professional even when faced with strange photographic requests.

■ **Ronnie Myers** at Magnolia Beauregard's Antiques in Asheville, North Carolina, who let us borrow some of his antique dress forms.

■ **Bari Caton**, for assisting with the writing of the first three chapters.

■ **Dana Irwin**, talented art director of many Lark books and a great book production partner.

■ **Pat Arcuri and Bernie Wolf**, for sharing their old family photos.

■ **Sally Hickerson** at Waechter's Silk Shop in Asheville, North Carolina, for making her store and its amazing collection of buttons available to us.

■ **Deborah Morgenthal** at Lark Books, for her editorial support and assistance.

■ **Bob Bowles**, my husband and best friend, for his encouragement and gift certificates to my favorite fabric shop.

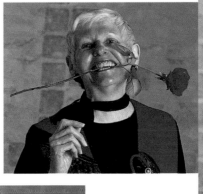

Index

A

Antique textiles 24, 83

Appliqué 56, 58, 62, 63, 67, 75, 84, 90, 110, 116

C

Closures 30

Collar treatments 30

Couching 84, 94, 120

Creativity

    closures 30

    collar treatments 40

Developing ideas 22

    design themes 34

D

Design themes 34

Detachable collar 98

E

Embroidery, machine 112

Evaluating your wardrobe 18

F

Fabric manipulation 65

Felting 51

Finishing 44

Fitting 37

Fleece, 58, 72, 103

M

Machine embroidery 112

Machine quilting 47, 108, 112

Marbling 70

Men's neckties 54

Microfiber 80

O

Organizing

    supplies 12

    time 15

P

Patterns, selecting for efficiency 36

Piecing 49, 54, 56, 79, 86, 88, 92, 102, 104, 105, 118, 121, 122

Pin-weaving 26

Prairie points 49

Puffing 61

Q

Quilting, machine 47, 108, 112

R

Reversible vest 108, 112, 121

S

Silk ribbon embroidery 93

Strip weaving 98, 114

Supplies, organizing 12

T

Tatting 93

Time, organizing 15

U

Upholstery fabric 95, 97

W

Wardrobe, evaluating 18